INDIA RESEARCH PRESS / TARA PRESS INTERNATIONAL

INDIA

Corporate Office -
B-4/22,Khajuraho - 110 029, INDIA
Telephone :   91-11-2369 4610 Telefax :   91-11-2471 8637

Editorial Office -

Flat #6, TRUST OFFICE - 110003, India.
Tel: 00.91.11.2469 4610, 2469 4855
TeleFAX: 00.91.11.24618637, 417 57 113

AMERICA

JSL INC Press.
14431 Ventura Blvd suite 538
Sherman Oaks CA 91423
www.hiddenmoon.com

Hecate I: Death, Transition and Spiritual Mastery

Foreword..5

I. Hecate...10

Hecate through Experience

Hecate's Spiritual Purpose

Hecate, the Origin of Terror

The Origin of Suffering

Story of Hecate Chthonia

Fear, the Real Darkness

Wheel of Hecate

Hecate and Finding our Natural Place

II. Death 46

The Illusion of Death

Death, the Next Great Experience

The Cordolium-Skull Meditation

III. Seven Caelums..59

The Black Sun

IV. The Power of Three..77

The Three Phases of Dying

The Three Faces of Death

The Untimely Dead

The Three Classes of Spirits

V. Roman Vicani..77

The Roman Vicani

Vagina, the New Buddha

Natural Darkness

Baphomet, Son of Hecate Nirvan

Obtaining God through the Lowest State

The Black Bliss

The Two Faces of Nature

The Problem with Light Consciousness

VI.	Pictures of Jade Sol Luna...100
VII.	Hecate's Forms 109
VIII.	Hecate Worship..125
IX.	Hecate Invocation..132
X.	Hecate Hymns...137
XI.	Hecate, The Goddess of Lunar Astrology........................148
XII.	Hecate in Literature..158
XIII.	The Mystic and Cerberus..184
XIV.	Hecate Art...208

This book is based upon the discourses taken from Jade Luna's seminars, **"Embracing Goddess as Destroyer"**, **"God Realization and the Path of the Dark Mother"**, **"La Sera"** and **"Astrologia Victoria"**.

Copyright 2008 JSL Press/Tarainternationalpress

When Jade Luna asked me to write the Foreword to his book about the Dark Mother/Hecate I was surprised since I consider myself a neophyte regarding this powerful primal Goddess. I'm a professional playwright whose work is being adapted to film and I teach Screenwriting at the University of New Mexico. Who am I to offer insights into a book by an adept like Jade whose spiritual experiences humble and open you to the soul's long and mysterious journey?

In 2003 I had my first astrological reading with Jade. Prior to this reading with him which shed much light on my path in this world, I had completed a production in Chicago of my play, **Final Angel. Final Angel** received unusual responses from the Chicago critics and won the ***After Dark Award*** for Outstanding New Work of 2003. The writing of this play which deals with a woman's literal journey into the Underworld shadowed my own personal experience. I suffered from out of the blue health problems, betrayals and enormous levels of personal fear as this play went from Santa Fe, New Mexico to a reading at the Actor's Studio in New York to the Chicago Stage. Like my heroine who undergoes a profound confrontation with the forces of her own dark side and via the unsettling ministrations of her therapist, Persephone Queen of the Dead, goes straight to uh, Hades...it seemed everyone associated with this play got a taste of something inexplicable.

What I learned from the comments of critics who referred more than once to how haunting the play was, my director who though quite experienced felt he was in over his head, and the actors and audience members, was that people hunger for illumination, true experience and an understanding of the meaning of human suffering. However, they are also drawn to the mysteries of the Underworld and this is the case even if their prime background is a more conservative Christianity.

The spiritual wisdom that Jade is now imparting comes as he always says by way of Hecate herself, the One whom the great being Ramakrishna said lead him to God realization. Jade maintains Hecate is the Great Destroyer behind the force which annihilates our fears. It is She who eliminates whatever keeps us from knowing God and experiencing Divine Love. Yet Hecate's history while rich and ancient, is basically misunderstood.

I have only to remember my days as an actress in Chicago when I played the Third Witch in Shakespeare's **Macbeth**. Hecate is portrayed as the Queen of Witches in **Macbeth** and has the final say in how Macbeth is to be dealt with. In our production Hecate was played by a pretty, plump girl from Skokie, Illinois whose portrayal transversed mild irritation with her witch's antics to an attempt at being 'scary.' Even then I recall feeling that Shakepeare's creation of Hecate was full of a menacing powerful grace and that as the Goddess of the

Crossroads, *he* seemed to know, *she* knew stuff. The Bard implies Hecate is in charge of both the night and karma, and it is well known that the Greek myths informed and inspired many Elizabethan writers. I remember I wanted to play Hecate myself and was deeply drawn to the power Shakespeare was unabashed about 'bestowing' on her. I am fairly sure though that both the actress who protrayed her and our modern audience saw Hecate as no more than a fun, Halloweenish spectacle.

So *who* is She? A being who can put the terror of the unknown into three wild, frightening witches, the one who witnessed the rape of Persephone in the Greek myths, or an actual living presence we are ignorant of in this time of spiritual hunger?

Jade will take us to an understanding of Hecate's true work on this planet if we can stay open and not reject his insights out of our own fears. Some of what Jade imparts might lead us to a harrowing place as there is an aspect to the spiritual journey he reveals that may shock fundamentalists of all kinds. Yet for anyone who yearns for deeper self-knowledge and an opening of the heart this book will be an essential gift on the path of the Divine Mother.

Since meeting Jade and listening to his lectures and meditating on Hecate, I have newly begun to walk with her. I am awed at how little I know of these deep mysteries and the hidden past of this extraordinary Deity. From the time I thought her merely a fantasy of the Bard's imagination or a creation of the Greek playwrights, I am moved now into a place of experience I could not have dreamed of.

Thanks to Jade and his devotion to the Dark Mother along with his tireless pursuit of the loneliest places few willingly traverse, many of us will have a door opened to us.

May the love of this greatly misunderstood, uniquely powerful path which leads the Soul to its final attainment be revealed to us now at a time when we need it most. - *Stephanie Kuehn*

There is only one God, but the one God manifests himself in a million different forms. The Angels, Gods and Arch Angels are nothing other than the different functions, personalities and duties of the one, although, they are individual. As human beings are also God, we as well, being individual, have our own responsibilities and duties. Hecate is the aspect of the one God that withers away the false self so the divine can be realized. This is my experience of the force of Natura (nature) called Hecate.

HECATE

Hecate, **Hekate** (*Hekátē*), or **Ekata** was originally a goddess of the wilderness and childbirth originating from Thrace, or among the Carians of Anatolia. Popular cults venerating her as a mother goddess integrated her persona into Greek culture as Ἑκάτη. In Ptolemaic Alexandria she ultimately achieved her connotations as a goddess of sorcery and her role as the 'Queen of Ghosts', in which guise she was transmitted to post-Renaissance culture. Today she is often seen as a goddess of witchcraft and Wicca. She is also the equivalent of the Roman Trivia. Her origin in the east is the Goddess Dhumavati, in this form Hecate is the Void of Nirvan.

> *The evidence of the monuments as to the character and significance of Hekate is almost as full as that of the literature. But it is only in the later period that they come to express her manifold and mystic nature. Before the fifth century there is little doubt that she was usually represented as of single form like any other divinity, and it was thus that the Boeotian poet imagined her, as nothing in his verses contains any allusion to a triple formed goddess. The earliest known monument is a small terracotta found in Athens, with a dedication to Hekate (Plate XXXVIII. a), in writing of the style of the sixth century. The goddess is seated on a throne with a chaplet bound round her head; she is altogether without attributes and character, and the only value of this work, which is evidently of quite a general type and gets a special reference and name merely from the inscription, is that it proves the single shape to be her earlier from, and her recognition at Athens to be earlier than the Persian invasion.*

Pausanias stated that Hecate was first depicted in triplicate by the sculptor Alkamenes in the Greek Classical period of the late 5th century. Some classical portrayals, such as the one illustrated below, show her as a triplicate goddess holding a torch, a key and a serpent. Others continue to depict her in singular form. In Egyptian-inspired Greek esoteric writings connected with Hermes Trismegistus, and in magical papyri of Late Antiquity she is described as having three heads: one dog, one serpent and one horse. Hecate's triplicity is expressed in a more Hellene fashion, with three bodies instead, where she is shown taking part in the battle with the Titans in the vast frieze of the great altar of Pergamum, now in Berlin. In the Argolid, near the shrine of the Dioscuri, the 2nd-century CE traveler Pausanias saw the temple of Hecate opposite the sanctuary of Eilethyia; "The image is a work of Scopas. This one is of stone, while the bronze images opposite, also of Hekate, were made respectively by Polycleitus and his brother Naucydes, son of Mothon. (*Description of Greece* ii.22.7)

A 4th c-entury BCE marble relief from Crannon in Thessaly was dedicated by a race-horse owner. It shows Hecate, with a hound beside her, placing a wreath on the head of a mare. This statue is in the British Museum, inventory number 816. Her attendant and animal representation is of a bitch, and the most common form of offering was to leave meat at a crossroads. Sometimes dogs themselves were sacrificed to her (a good indication of her non-Hellenic origin, as dogs along with donkeys, very rarely played this role in genuine Greek ritual).

In *Argonautica*, a third century BCE Alexandrian epic based on early materials, Jason placates Hecate in a ritual prescribed by Medea: bathed at midnight in a stream of flowing water, and dressed in dark robes, Jason is to dig a pit and offer a libation of honey and blood from the throat of a sheep, which was set on a pyre by the pit and wholly consumed as a holocaust, then retreat from the site without looking back (*Argonautica*, iii). All these elements betoken the rites owed to a chthonic deity.

Mythology

Despite popular belief, Hecate was not originally a Greek goddess. She is unknown to Homer and in fact the earliest written references to her are in Hesiod's *Theogony*. The place of origin of her cult is uncertain, but it is thought that she had popular cult followings in Thrace. Her most important sanctuary was Lagina, a theocratic city-state in which the goddess was served by eunuchs. Lagina, where the famous temple of Hecate drew great festal assemblies every year, lay close to the originally Macednian colony of Straonikea. In Thrace she played a role similar to that of lesser-Hermes, namely a governess of liminal points and the wilderness, bearing little resemblance to the night-walking crone. Additionally, this led to her role of aiding women in childbirth and the raising of young men.

There was a fane sacred to Hecate as well in the precincts of the Temple of Artemis at Ephesus, where the eunuch priests, *megabyzi*, officiated. Hesiod records that she was among the offspring of Gaia and Uranus, the Earth and Sky. In *Theogony* he ascribed to Hecate such wide-ranging and fundamental powers, that it is hard to resist seeing such a deity as a figuration of the Great Goddess, though as a good Olympian Hesiod ascribes her powers as the "gift" of Zeus:

> *"Hecate whom Zeus the son of Cronos honoured above all. He gave her splendid gifts, to have a share of the earth and the unfruitful sea. She received honor also in starry heaven, and is honored exceedingly by the deathless gods.... The son of Cronos did her no wrong nor took anything away of all that was her portion among the former Titan gods: but she holds, as the division was at the first from the beginning, privilege both in earth, and in heaven, and in sea".*

Her gifts towards mankind are all-encompassing, Hesiod tells:

> *"Whom she will she greatly aids and advances: she sits by worshipful kings in judgment, and in the assembly whom her will is distinguished among the people. And when men arm themselves for the battle that destroys men, then the goddess is at hand to give victory and grant glory readily to whom she will. Good is she also when men contend at the games, for there too the goddess is with them and profits them: and he who by might and strength gets the victory wins the rich prize easily with joy, and brings glory to his parents. And she is good to stand by horsemen, whom she will: and to those whose business is in the grey discomfortable sea, and who pray to Hecate and the loud-crashing Earth-Shaker, easily the glorious*

goddess gives great catch, and easily she takes it away as soon as seen, if so she will. She is good in the byre with Hermes to increase the stock. The droves of kine and wide herds of goats and flocks of fleecy sheep, if she will, she increases from a few, or makes many to be less".

Hecate was carefully attended:

"For to this day, whenever any one of men on earth offers rich sacrifices and prays for favour according to custom, he calls upon Hecate. Great honour comes full easily to him whose prayers the goddess receives favourably, and she bestows wealth upon him; for the power surely is with her".

Hesiod emphasizes that Hecate was an only child, the daughter of Asteria, a star-goddess who was the sister of Leto, the mother of Artemis and Apollo. Grandmother of the three cousins was Phoebe the ancient Titaness who personified the moon. Hecate was a reappearance of Phoebe, a moon goddess herself, who appeared in the dark of the moon.

His inclusion and praise of Hecate in *Theogony* is troublesome for scholars in that he seems fulsomely to praise her attributes and responsibilities in the ancient cosmos even though she is both relatively minor and foreign. It is theorized that Hesiod's original village had a substantial Hecate following and that his inclusion of her in the Theogony was his own way to boost the home-goddess for unfamiliar hearers.

As her cult spread into areas of Greece it presented a conflict, as Hecate's role was already filled by other more prominent gods in the Greek pantheon, above all by Artemis, and by more archaic figures, such as Nemesis.

There are two versions of Hecate that emerge in Greek myth. The lesser role integrates Hecate while not diminishing Artemis. In this version Hecate is a mortal priestess who is commonly associated with Iphigeneia and scorns and insults Artemis, eventually leading to her suicide. Artemis then adorns the dead body with jewelry and whispers for her spirit to rise and become her Hecate, and act similar to Nemesis as an avenging spirit, but solely for injured women. Such myths where a home god sponsors or 'creates' a foreign god were widespread in ancient cultures as a way of integrating foreign cults. Additionally, as Hecate's cult grew, her figure was added to the myth of the birth of Zeus as one of the midwives that hid the child, while Cronus consumed the deceiving rock handed to him by Gaia.

The second version helps to explain how Hecate gains the title of the "Queen of Ghosts" and her role as a goddess of sorcery. Similar to totems of Hermes—*herms*— placed at borders as a ward against danger, images of Hecate, as a liminal goddess, could also serve in such a protective role. It became common to place statues of the goddess at the gates of cities, and eventually domestic doorways. Over time, the association of keeping out evil spirits led to the belief that if offended Hecate could also let in evil spirits. Thus invocations to Hecate arose as her the supreme governess of the borders between the normal world and the spirit world.

Eventually, Hecate's power resembled that of sorcery. Medea, who was a priestess of Hecate, used witchcraft in order to handle magic herbs and poisons with skill, and to be able to stay the course of rivers, or check the paths of the stars and the moon.

Implacable Hecate has been called "tender-hearted", a euphemism perhaps to emphasize her concern with the disappearance of Persephone, when she addressed Demeter with sweet words when the goddess was distressed.

Although she was never truly incorporated among the Olympian gods, the modern understanding of Hecate is derived from the syncretic Hellenistic culture of Alexandria. In the magical papyri of Ptolemaic Egypt, she is called the she-dog or bitch, and her presence is signified by the barking of dogs. She sustained a large following as a goddess of protection and childbirth. In late imagery she also has two ghostly dogs as servants by her side.

In modern times Hecate has become a prevalent figure in feminist-inspired Neopagan religions, and a version of Hecate has been appropriated by Wicca and other modern magic-practicing traditions.

Relations in the Greek Pantheon

Hecate is a pre-Olympian chthonic goddess. The Greek sources do not offer a story of her parentage, beyond the

Theogony, or of her relations in the Greek pantheon: Sometimes Hecate is a Titaness, daughter of Perses and Asteria, and a mighty helper and protector of mankind. Her continued presence was explained by asserting that, because she was the only Titan that aided Zeus in the battle of gods and Titans, she was not banished into the underworld realms after their defeat by the Olympians.

It is also told that she is the daughter of Demeter or Pheraia. Hecate, like Demeter, was a goddess of the earth and fertility. Sometimes she is called a daughter of Zeus.

Like many ancient mother or earth-goddesses she remains unmarried and has no regular consort. On the other side she is the mother of many monsters, such as Scylla.

Other names and epithets

- **Chthonian** (Earth/Underworld goddess)
- **Crataeis** (the Mighty One)
- **Enodia** (Goddess of the paths)
- **Antania** (Enemy of mankind)
- **Kurotrophos** (Nurse of the Children and Protectress of mankind)
- Artemis of the crossroads
- **Propylaia** (the one before the gate)
- **Propolos** (the attendant who leads)
- **Phosphoros** (the light-bringer)
- **Soteira** ("Saviour")
- **Prytania** (invincible Queen of the Dead)
- **Trioditis** (gr.) **Trivia** (latin: Goddess of Three Roads)
- **Klêidouchos** (Keeper of the Keys)

- **Tricephalus** or **Triceps** (The Three-Headed)

Goddess of the crossroads

Hecate had a special role at three-way crossroads, where the Greeks set poles with masks of each of her heads facing different directions

The crossroad aspect of Hecate stems from her original sphere as a goddess of the wilderness and untamed areas. This led to sacrifice in order for safe travel into these areas. This role is similar to lesser Hermes, that is, a god of liminal points or boundaries.

Hecate is the Greek version of *Trivia* "the three ways" in Roman mythology. Eligius in the 7th century CE reminded his recently converted flock in Flanders "No Christian should make or render any devotion to the gods of the trivium, where three roads meet, to the fanes or the rocks, or springs or groves or corners", acts the Druids often did.

Goddess of sorcery

The goddess of sorcery or magic is Hecate's most common modern title. Hecate was the goddess who appeared most often in magical texts such as the Greek Magical Papyri and curse tablets, along with Hermes.

Emblems

Traditionally, Hecate is represented as carrying torches, very often has a knife, and may appear holding a rope, a key, a phial, flowers, or a pomegranate.

The torch is presumably a symbol of the light that illuminates the darkness, as the Greeks secured Hecate in her role as the bringer of wisdom. Her knife represents her role as midwife in cutting the umbilical cord (possibly symbolized by the rope), as well as severing the link between the body and spirit at death. The key is significant to Hecate's role as gatekeeper, being the one who could open the doors to sacred knowledge. The Orphic Hymns list her as the "keybearing Queen of the entire Cosmos." The pomegranate was seen by the Ancient Greeks as the fruit of the underworld, though it was also used as a love-gift between Greek men and women. This may be because a pomegranate was eaten by Persephone, binding her to the underworld and to Hades.

In the so-called "Chaldean Oracles" that were edited in Alexandria, she was also associated with a serpentine maze around a spiral, known as Hecate's wheel (the "Strophalos of Hecate", verse 194 of Isaac Preston Cory's 1836 translation). The symbolism referred to the serpent's power of rebirth, to the labyrinth of knowledge through which Hecate could lead mankind, and to the flame of life itself: "The life-producing bosom of Hecate, that Living Flame which clothes itself in Matter to manifest Existence" (verse 55 of Cory's translation of the Chaldean Oracles).

Animals

The she-dog is the animal most commonly associated with Hecate. She was sometimes called the 'Black she-dog' and black dogs were once sacrificed to her in purification rituals. At Colophon in Thrace, Hecate might be manifest as a dog. The sound of barking dogs was the first sign of her approach in Greek and Roman literature. The frog, significantly a creature that can cross between two elements, is also sacred to Hecate. As a triple goddess, she sometimes appears with three heads-one each of a dog, horse, and bear or of dog, serpent and lion.

During the Medieval period in western Europe, Hecate was reverenced by witches who adopted parts of her mythos as their goddess of sorcery. Because Hecate had already been much maligned by the late Roman period, Christians of the era found it easy to vilify her image. Thus were all her creatures also considered "creatures of darkness"; however, the history of creatures such as ravens, night-owls, snakes, scorpions, asses, bats, horses, bears, and lions as her creatures is not always a dark and frightening one.

Plants and herbs

The yew, cypress, hazel, black poplar, cedar, and willow are all sacred to Hecate.

The leaves of the black poplar are dark on one side and light on the other, symbolizing the boundary between the worlds. The yew has long been associated with the Underworld.

The yew has strong associations with death as well as rebirth. A poison prepared from the seeds was used on arrows, and yew wood was commonly used to make bows and dagger hilts. The potion in Hecate's cauldron contains 'slips of yew'. Yew berries carry Hecate's power, and can bring wisdom or death. The seeds are highly poisonous, but the fleshy, coral-colored 'berry' surrounding it is not. If prepared correctly, the berry can cause visual hallucinations (Ratsch).

Many other herbs and plants are associated with Hecate, including garlic, almonds, lavender, thyme, myrrh, mugwort, cardamon, mint, dandelion, hellebore, and lesser celandine. Several poisons and hallucinogens are linked to Hecate, including belladonna, hemlock, mandrake, aconite (known as hecateis), and opium poppy. Many of Hecate's plants were those that can be used shamanistically to achieve varyings states of consciousness.

Places

Wild areas, forests, borders, city walls and doorways, crossroads, and graveyards are all associated with Hecate.

It is often stated that the moon is sacred to Hecate. This is argued against by Farnell (1896, p.4):

> *Some of the late writers on mythology, such as Cornutus and Cleomedes, and some of the modern, such as Preller and the writer in Roscher's Lexicon and Petersen, explain the three figures as symbols of the three phases of the moon. But very little can be said in favour of this, and very much against it. In the first place, the statue of Alcamenes represented Hekate Επιπυργιδια, whom the Athenian of that*

period regarded as the warder of the gate of his Acropolis, and as associated in this particular spot with the Charites, deities of the life that blossoms and yields fruit. Neither in this place nor before the door of the citizen's house did she appear as a lunar goddess.

We may also ask, why should a divinity who was sometimes regarded as the moon, but had many other and even more important connexions, be given three forms to mark the three phases of the moon, and why should Greek sculpture have been in this solitary instance guilty of a frigid astronomical symbolism, while Selene, who was obviously the moon and nothing else, was never treated in this way? With as much taste and propriety Helios might have been given twelve heads.

However in the magical papyri of Greco-Roman Egypt there survive several hymns which identify Hecate with Selene and the moon, extolling her as supreme Goddess, mother of the gods. In this form, as a threefold goddess, Hecate continues to have followers in some neopagan religions.

Festivals

Hecate was worshipped by both the Greeks and the Romans who had their own festivals dedicated to her. According to Ruickbie (2004:19) the Greeks observed two days sacred to Hecate, one on the 13th of August and one on the 30th of November, whilst the Romans observed the 29th of every month as her sacred day.

Cross-cultural parallels

The figure of Hecate can often be associated with the figure of Isis in Egyptian myth, mainly due to her role as sorceress. In Hebrew myth she is often compared to the figure of Lilith and the Whore of Babylon in later Christian tradition. Both were symbols of liminal points, and Lilith also has a role in sorcery. Some scholars ultimately compare her to the Virgin Mary.

Before she became associated with Greek mythology, she had many similarities with Artemis (wilderness, and watching over wedding ceremonies) and Hera (child rearing and the protection of young men or heroes, and watching over wedding ceremonies).

Hecate in modern magic

This article or section does not cite its **references or sources.**

In modern times, Hecate has become popular in Neopaganism and Wicca, largely due to her association as the goddess of sorcery. Hecate can take numerous roles. As a goddess of magic, she not seen as exclusively benevolent, and her bestowal of favor is often seen as fickle. Punishments meted out to those who displease her are held to include inflicting madness in some cases, or sickness, poisoning, and disease in others. However Hecate is not primarily malevolent, and to those in her favor she is thought to grant boons, including relief from pain, ease in childbirth, and the curing of disease and physical ailments.

Worship of Hecate can take many forms. In some cases animal sacrifices have been alleged. Most modern pagans actively discourage the practice of animal sacrifice. Common forms of worship include prostration, chanting adoration for Hecate, fasting, the collecting of lanterns, the burning of oils and incense, and the burning of bread and other foods as sacrifices.

Some groups worship Artemis instead due to Hecate's supposedly fickle nature and lack of benevolence. Other gods commonly worshipped by such groups are Theia and Hyperion. Some Neopagans worship Artemis, Selene and Hecate as a kind of trinity, representing maiden (Artemis), mother (Selene) and crone (Hecate), and also the various phases of the moon (crescent, full and new, respectively).

In some modern pagan beliefs, wild animals are sacred to Hecate. However, creatures of darkness — such as ravens, crows, owls, and snakes — are most commonly used. Dragons are also included, as Hecate and her legendary priestess Medea were both said to ride chariots pulled by dragons. Several images of Hecate show her holding a snake. Snakes have long been connected with chthonic powers and the powers of life, death, and rebirth (see Serpent).

Queen of ghosts

Queen of Ghosts is a title associated with Hecate due to the belief that she can both prevent harm from leaving, but also allow harm to enter from the spirit world. Hecate thus has a role and special power in graveyards and at crossroads. She guards the "ways and paths that cross". Her association with graveyards also played a large part in the idea of Hecate as a lunar goddess.

Hecate through Experience

It is not your light that reincarnates, it is your dark. If you do not become conscious of your shadow, you will reincarnate until you do. Hecate is the force that makes you conscious of your shadow.- Jade Sol Luna

Hecate's Spiritual Purpose
*note-Caelum means "inner heaven" and is explained on page 59

Hecate is the Goddess that removes the impressions that prevent us from merging into the Divine. Hecate is the Mother of the Night and we, as human beings, could not spiritually progress without her. What makes Hecate such an immense force is that she exists in the lowest forms as well as in the highest. SHE has no duality and experiences herself as "the Everything". At the end of the journey, when its time for the soul to return to Sol Caelum (the Realm of Oneness), SHE is the final force that removes the last impression inside the mind, which usually prevents complete unity. SHE is the great mystery (TRIVIA), the experience, the Power of God that separates, binds, creates and removes. Hecate is the breath of existence. Without a Goddess like Hecate, the spiritual path would lack inspiration or movement. SHE is the One that shakes us up on earth because her motive is to reunite us with God.

Hecate's image has greatly changed through time. SHE was originally the Goddess of Darkness, but how the human mind views "Darkness" now and in ancient time is very different. Originally, darkness was the force that created the suffering needed in order to advance one on the spiritual path. Without suffering, there is no desire to experience the Divine. SHE is the Mother that grabs you by the ear and says that it's time to wake up and come home. SHE is the form of the Mother that grants the realization of God. If someone embarks on the path of God Realization, they are passed over to one of the major forms of Hecate. Hecate is the REMOVER of karma and it is through her that the highest plane is achieved.

There are innumerable forms of the Dark Mother, but the form that brings the disciple "Karmic Awareness" is Hecate. As it was known in ancient times, the one that obtains the awareness of "Hecate" can experience awareness in every state. Hecate is the most difficult form of the Dark Mother meaning that the work of Hecate as a Goddess is the most challenging in the human experience. Hecate is in everything, the high and the low and it is easier to experience her in her softer forms. Embracing her in the more difficult forms like Hecate Chthonia requires breaking the mind away from the rational. The Saint, the Sinner, the Good, the Bad, the Light, the Dark...are all a part of God and Hecate is the force that allows different aspects of God to be experienced in her totality. Once God is realized in every state, the journey is complete. Hecate is in every state of consciousness, to know her in her totality is to know God. Hecate was the original force that created creation. Hindus call this Adi Shakti, the first primal power that started the universe.

The Origin of Terror

Before creation, God existed alone as an ocean of total Sat-Chit-Ananda (knowledge, power and bliss). In the beginning, this all powerful ocean existed in a state of unconsciousness (meaning He could not use these forces consciously). The second that God had the thought of becoming conscious of Himself, the Dark Mother Hecate was born. Hecate, at the moment of Her birth created the whole universe and then returned back to the ocean of God (Vishnu Pad) and sprung forth the individualized drops of the ocean through the web of her creation. Human beings are individual drops of the divine ocean of God. The job of Hecate is to return us back to the ocean of God, but conscious of the self as opposed to unconscious, as we were in the beginning. Hecate is the force that moves us back to the divine self.

How does Hecate move us through the web of creation? She moves us through suffering. Suffering removes us from all the desires that keep us from manifesting our true self. Suffering destroys the urge for individual existence or, in other words, our pride. I am commonly asked or debated about the topic of suffering in my seminars. The usual comment from attendees is the statement that "happiness creates unity and suffering creates separation". It requires suffering to take us out of our small self and to tune us up with the larger self. Without suffering, human beings would desire to reincarnate for eternity. It is the force of suffering that makes us desire to unify or to return back to the ocean of God.

In ancient mysticism, suffering has a more difficult side called "terror". In Ancient Greece, Hecate was commonly titled, the "Queen of Terror" or "Queen of Night Terrors". One might ask what terror has to do with the spiritual path? We must look at where terror comes from in order to embrace it. So, where does terror or fear come from? Before the beginning of time, we were in a blissful state of unconsciousness until we were suddenly awakened from our unconscious bliss by Hecate to move us through the web of creation.

Being pushed out of the unconscious ocean set an imprint of complete terror (like a child being separated from his/her mother). Terror comes from the fear of being brutally torn from our comfort zone and those things that create the illusion of earthly safety and security. That force of being pushed out of the ocean was so deep that it far supersedes the fear of death, loss, loneliness and losing a loved one, as these energies are just the shadow of that first push out of our unconscious bliss into creation. Buddhists have a word for her in this form, they call her "The Void".

Just before we return back to the ocean of God consciously we have to go through the "void of terror" consciously. This terror is different because instead of being pushed out of the ocean (the first terror), we have to return back to the ocean and the terror now is about *losing the false self to unite with the divine self.* So, it is our duty to return back to the ocean *but with full consciousness.*

Hecate, the Origin of Suffering

After creation began and human life started to flourish, Zeus (the Christian Father, Ruler of Heaven) was crowned "King of the Gods". In the beginning time, human life was very peaceful, there was absolutely no suffering and humans would live for hundreds, if not thousands of years. After the very first human age ended, Zeus decided to review the first cycle of human existence and upon this reflection, realized that humans were not evolving spiritually. After the death of each human, they would desire to return and reincarnate back to Earth. This started to disturb Zeus, because he was aware that the goal of creation and life was to return back to Sol Caelum (The Realm of Love and Light). Out of his frustration with humans lack of desire to return home, Zeus created rules and decided that humans would have to pay for their bad actions (bad actions were originally the selfish actions you took to gratify the separate self). After great thought, Zeus created Tartarus (the Realm called Hell) and instructed all the Gods and Angels to tell humans that they would have to suffer in the "afterlife" if they did not use human life for the realization of returning to Sol Caelum. After the creation of Tartarus, Zeus asked all the angels if there was one that would be interested in ruling over Tartarus and the Underworld. None responded. He came to the conclusion that the only two beings capable of this task, was either himself or his brother (of Wealth), Hades. Hades, when originally asked to rule the Underworld, declined, but after realizing where his true power lie, accepted the job and his title as "King of the Underworld". Eons of time passed and Hades began to recognize that humans were still not evolving and that punishment in the "afterlife" was not sufficient for humans to maintain the goal of realization and the return to Sol Caelum. Life was too easy and humans chose to block out the voices of the Gods and Tartarus altogether. Out of compassion, Hades saw that the only way to make humans consciously aware of inner bliss (caelums), was to make them suffer in the present human world for their bad actions (remember in the beginning, humans only suffered in the "afterlife"). The moment Hades had that thought, Hecate, Queen of the Night and Terror, was born on earth. (Hecate originally resided in Nirvan and Death). The ground shook, the stars smiled and the winds howled throughout the planet! Even Zeus went into awe at this Queen's majesty. Hecate, the reason for all creation, was now present throughout the whole planet and was given power over the Earth, Sky and Sea. She immediately claimed her children, called them witches and dressed them in black. These children were blessed with knowing the riddle of creation (Hecate's Roman name is Trivia). Human beings, through the greatness of Hecate, were now responsible for their bad actions while they were alive. If Zeus and Hades could not make human beings desire to return back to God (Sol Caelum), Hecate could!

The Reason for Suffering

Without suffering, human beings would desire to reincarnate for all eternity. The goal of human life is to return home. There are various types of suffering that a human being has to go through. The first type of suffering is called "self created suffering". Self created suffering comes from our own actions. Every action we take to gratify the false self creates a reaction of earthly suffering. After our karma is balanced then we have to deal with "Godly Suffering". Godly suffering deals with taking on the karma of those around you. A person getting ready for the Caelums does not suffer for their actions but for those close to them. Taking on the energy of others is a theme for those that connect to the astral worlds (astral worlds are between earth and the Caelums). When a selected person starts to go through the Caelums, they suffer for the whole of creation. They have no more ties or connections to the earth plane and the Great Mother Hecate gives them some of her work.

The goal of spirituality is to make people strong enough to handle the greater path. If one does not have the ability to handle the suffering of life, a weakness is created that does not allow a person to move through the Caelums. The worship of Hecate gives one an enormous inner strength to handle the massive experience of God. Hecate's main home is Nirvan (The Void), and when you invoke her you are dragging the energy of Nirvan in your heart. This invocation alone, if done sincerely can start to prepare the person for handling the Caelums. We as human beings all have love, but only very few have the strength to handle the Goddess in her totality.

Story of Hecate Chthonia – Goddess of the Underworld

After Zeus passed out all the wonderful duties to the other gods and goddesses, there Hecate stood at the end of the line. Zeus said, "My Black Queen, I give you the duty of suffering, grief and annihilation." After this assignment, all the gods and goddesses abandoned her, including Zeus and she was left with NOTHING. She could not rely on anyone or anything, but the utter darkness of the VOID. She had to stand alone with no support. After eons of time, her pain and suffering turned to love, her grief turned to strength and her annihilation (widowhood) turned to freedom. *"Hecate is the embodiment of sorrow, She is the wisdom of death, She is the bliss of annihilation-how will you greet her when She comes to your door?"* (Quote from Jade's seminar, "Embracing the Goddess as Destroyer").

Hecate is the deity that shows up at the moment of pain, suffering, grief, loss, trauma and all difficult transitions. Out of all the forms of the Goddess, Hecate Chthonia may be the most difficult one to embrace because her work is so utterly human. She is the dark side of the moon that is involved in all the difficulties a person will have to face, including emotional ones. Hecate Chthonia lives in grief, fear, depression, wrath, lust and annihilation. Although her work on Earth is so intense, she is known in Ancient Greece to be very loving and one of her titles is "The Tender-Hearted One". Interestingly enough, this title is also given to her Hindu form as Dhumavati, the Widow Goddess. *Dhumavati is a widow sitting in an unhitched chariot, therefore, "a woman going nowhere, the ultimate symbol of all that is unlucky, unattractive and inauspicious" (Ibid, 182). Sometimes, though, she is presented as attractive, in which case she embodies the most threatening of women in Hindu society, for young widows are believed to be "driven by unsatisfied sexual longings without reason to resist" (Ibid, 190).*

Hecate (in her Chthonia form) carries a buffalo horn in her left hand representing her service to the Lord Hades (the God of the Dead and the Underworld) and her direction is in the southwest. Her Chthonia form is one of sheer terror. She makes up the terrible Underworld trinity with Persephone and Hades. She lights up the night with loss, separation, divorce, crime, death and presides at the scenes of car accidents, crime, cemeteries, hospitals, haunted houses and the desolate desert. Hecate is present at your birth and arranges all the difficult things in your life based on your previous life actions. Nothing bad, wrong or evil is happening in one's life...just the reaping of what one sows. Hecate Chthonia holds the highest wisdom...which is "nothing bad ever happens, only our karma coming back to us." If there was ever a Goddess that intimately earns the phrase "karma is a bitch", it is the Queen Hecate in her Chthonia form!

So, why would anyone worship such a Goddess? Hecate Chthonia creates a disillusionment and disinterest in the ordinary average daily existence and she creates need for one to spend a great deal of time in solitude and internal space. She awakens the yogic principles of renunciation and more than anything, she teaches us that life is an illusion. Strength, compassion, psychic abilities and love are her inner qualities and she showers these on her devotees. She knows the realization of the self is the only reason for life and this is engrained in anyone strong enough to embrace such a Goddess Queen!

Fear, The Real Darkness

In order for the spirit to realize the soul, it has to BALANCE all of its karma. This is why, technically, humanity does not need to "wake up", for individuals are waking up gradually through the process of experience. Those who are trying to rush the awakening are holding onto control and fear. If, in one life, a woman chooses to become a nun, she may whitewash or repress her instincts (unless she has made this choice through love, not through the belief of good or bad). This will result in her taking the opposite interests (as a prostitute) in her next life to break out of the shell that prevented her from seeing the other aspects of who she is. It is not our conscious mind that takes rebirth, but our subconscious mind that does and every aspect of the subconscious has to become conscious for the souls realization. That is why the goal of ancient Celtic, ancient Greek and Tantra traditions is to focus on making the subconscious conscious and why the focus on darkness is of such grave importance. Darkness is perfectly descriptive in its name. It means: what you cannot see. If you neglect to look at or resist darkness, you have already fallen to it. Fear is the reason a person cannot look at themselves. Fear is the real darkness! If you do not understand your darkness, you will fail to it over and over again. I am not talking about anything evil; I am talking about being truly conscious of ALL of your self.

Hecate is my Mother Night, dance with the night, sit in the truth of death and the unknown. It's ok…life is a dream from which we must wake up. Someday you will be strong enough to love *all of God*, not just the obvious or simplistic ways that one does. Those that understand the beauty of darkness already have a head start. It is easy to embrace light, such as when a man loves a beautiful woman. Embracing that which is ugly or hidden is much harder and requires much more strength. The goal of life is self-realization and to love God in every aspect. God is the Yin and Yang both. Just because we do not like something, does not mean it is not God. For those who love the night, not by choice, but purely by nature, are opening to truth.

For me personally, I only live by one rule which is to "Harm No One"! I am free to unwind myself without fear or judgment of myself or others. Those who only focus on light are only experiencing one aspect of God. God is Non-Duality, He is the light and the dark, Hecate is the good and the bad (and beyond both), He is the splendor of the sun and She is the love of the moonless night. Someday, just try to open your heart and to love ALL of God.

Wheel of Hecate

Ancient mysticism from Italy to Ireland embraced the more difficult and challenging aspects of life as the highest of all gurus. For, it is thru life and its challenges that we unravel the truth of who we really are. The more difficult aspects can show up as emotions or experiences associated with the shadow self or the six energies that exist around the Heart Chakra. The Wheel of Hecate was a specific path that embraced *the dark* and dealt with working with the shadow self, as a means of self-knowledge on the path to God Realization. Whereas modern religions cast out the darkness, deny these energies and encourage renunciation of them (because of their inability to endure it), ancient Hecate devotees embraced the dark with the goal of realization. The Heart Center (Chakra) is the domain of this form of mysticism and Hecate is the Queen of this practice. The heart is one of the most difficult places to reside because the heart is the place of both pleasure and pain. When someone falls in love, they do not always experience joy. Most religions run directly to the Crown Chakra (the mind) for the light and peace of this chakra, but the realization of the self comes from the Heart Chakra. At the time of realization, the Heart Chakra opens the Crown Chakra and the Soma (nectar) of the crown drips into the Heart Chakra, then the self as God is realized. When someone starts to live through their Heart Chakra, an overwhelming amount of pain from previous births and this life may be present. With The Wheel of Hecate, the practice is to sit through these energies which will start to annihilate the false self. *On the other side of the shadows of the heart is the manifestation of the divine self.*

There are six shadows (the six-points located in the center of Hecate's Wheel which reflect the six main desires that prevent realization, and the three spokes around the six points reflect the three worlds of gross, subtle and mental) that exist around the Heart Chakra and an ancient mystic worked with and through these energies. The Goddess, women and love reflect the Heart Chakra and the shadows. In Roman mysticism, they did not feel self-realization was possible without the knowledge of the six shadows of the heart. The goal of understanding Hecate's Wheel is to move these energies into higher channels and bring them into consciousness to realize the self.

The six shadows of Hecate's Wheel around the heart are:
Pride
Sloth
Greed
Lust
Anger
Fear (Fear is the root of them. Mystics must approach this one first!)

Inside of each shadow is the origin for the existence of that shadow.

Pride comes from knowing that you are God.
Sloth (Christian gluttony) comes from knowing how hard the path is.
Greed comes from not feeling supported by God.
Lust comes from the desire to unify with your higher self.
Anger comes from not getting want you want.
Fear comes from the need to hold onto the false, separate self.

In working with these six shadows, the main purpose is to become conscious of them without indulging in them. If you indulge in them, you will experience Hecate's reaction to them.
If you indulge in *Pride*, you will become lonely.
If you indulge in *Sloth*, you will become spiritually dry.
If you indulge in *Greed*, you will have to become poor.
If you indulge in *Lust*, you will lose your divine center.
If you indulge in *Anger*, you will have to experience regret.
If you indulge in *Fear*, you will lose your strength.

The main practice of Hecate's Wheel is the middle path, where one pulls these energies up to the surface (of consciousness) and works with them without indulging in them. How does one begin to work with these energies? Worshipping Hecate and meditating on Hecate's Wheel is sufficient. She will start to bring these energies into consciousness, and she will use your life as the medium of this work. The Mother is a Divine Guru. If you devote yourself to her, she will take the role of a guru and teach you strength and love.

But there is a warning... There is no rest for those who are on the path. If you want peace, run to the Crown Chakra (the Mind), here there is safety. Remember, those who have earned peace of the Crown Chakra will someday be pulled back onto the path of God Realization through the love and annihilation of the Heart Chakra. The safety one seeks will be there when the highest level of love has been achieved, which is God Realization.

Impermanence

Impermanence is one of the essential doctrines of ancient mysticism. According to it, everything is constantly in flux. This changing flux excludes nothing-- even planets, stars and Gods. This is embodied in human life in the aging process and the cycle of birth and rebirth, and in any experience of loss; because things are impermanent, attachment to them is futile, and leads to suffering. The only true end is the realization of the self. Self realization/Mukti is the one reality which knows of no change, decay or death. Life is a process of evolution, but the spiritual path is a process of involution. You have to let go of who you think you are in order to realize the divine self. The divine self is free from illusion, delusion, decay and bondage. The Dark Mother is not for those who want to learn, she is for those who want to unlearn, to realize the secret of inner truth. Here is another phrase from the Latin epic OVID: "Hecate devotees sit amongst the Graves in Cemeteries, covered in bones with wisdom of Death, Herbs and Magic." These mystics were not evil, but they knew that the only purpose of life was to transcend this false reality for the greater reality (i.e. the subtle and mental realms). They knew they had to transcend the Seven Veils to experience the Goddess as the God-Head. Here are the Seven Veils that a witch must cross before the realization of the Goddess as God. (Note: Caelum means LOKA in Sanskrit).

(1) Saturnus Caelum- The First Awakening

(2) Jove Caelum, The Realm of Fairies/Ganas- The First Enlightenment

(3) Mavors Caelum- The Master Occultist

(4) Venus Caelum- Realm of Power, this realm was the goal of the ancient mystic, at this point the mystic, through the intoxication of love, could manifest major miracles.

(5) Mercius Caelum- The Realm of Pure Knowledge

(6) Luna Caelum -The Realm of Diana and Spiritual Intoxication, she would drown you in an ocean of wine and love.

(7) Sol Caelum- The merging of the spirit into the ocean of light, the end of reincarnation.

Hecate and finding our natural place

Life is a process of unfolding one's self, to find where you are the most natural with who you are. We instinctively commit to things that we feel we are at the moment, but in the end the opposite is revealed. A human being has to go through cycles of commitment to understand the truth of his/her inner self. As difficult as it is, when the
rug is pulled from underneath our feet, it is that jolt that removes the false self to then reveal what is the true natural self. Hecate, the fierce form of the Dark Mother, has the unfortunate grace of pulling the rug from underneath your feet and pulling you closer to your natural self.

She places you in situations that are not entirely natural for you so you will be strong in your real self when that time comes. After having the rug pulled from underneath us enough times, we start to make choices from a place of complete naturalness, not from the concept of good and bad.

After years of ruination (the removing of the false self), we start opening to our higher self. When we live in our higher self, we still have to suffer, but that suffering comes from the Great Mother using us for her particular duties. Self inflicted suffering is far more difficult than suffering that which comes from living in your higher self. The goal of spiritual practice is to awaken to the pure state of naturalness. One of the most difficult aspects of unifying with your higher self is letting go of being accepted. It is impossible to become your self and to impress everyone. God is far too diverse for that. If you are making everyone happy, you are doing something wrong. When you function from the space of naturalness you see how everyone is ONE in the Divine Mother's diversity. In short, Hecate's duty is to show us who we are by showing us what we are not. Without the rug being pulled from underneath our feet, we could never manifest our highest self. The goal of life is union, and we are all going to have to go through the suffering to get there. It is important to remember that life is a dream that we all must wake up from whether we like it or not. And thanks to Hecate, the potential for mastery is on the other side of the dream.

DEATH

The Illusion of Death

According to mystical experience, there are seven worlds in the universe (eight if you include Terra Caelum, earth). The seven worlds are Saturnus Caelum, Jove Caelum, Mavors Caelum, Venus Caelum, Mercurius Caelum, Luna Caelum, and Sol Caelum. The gross plane (Terra Caelum) is the earth where we dwell, while Jove Caelum is the celestial world to which people go after death to enjoy the reward of their positive actions on earth. Saturnus Caelum is the region between the two. Mercurius Caelum, Luna Caelum, and Sol Caelum constitute the light or mental planes, or the highest heavens, where advanced souls enjoy spiritual communion with the personal God or Goddess. On Jove Caelum, both heaven and hell exist. In the farthest region of Jove Caelum, souls that have created too much negative karma sojourn after death and reap the results of their negative actions on earth. Thus, from the viewpoint of the mystic, heaven and hell are merely different worlds, bound by time, space, and causality. According to ancient mysticism, desires are responsible for a person's embodiment. Some of these desires can best be fulfilled in a human body, and some in a celestial body. Accordingly, a soul's physical body is determined by its unfulfilled desires and the results of its past actions. A celestial body is for reaping the results of past karma, not for performing actions to acquire a new body. We only create karma in a human body, because only human beings do good or bad consciously. Human birth is therefore a great experience, for in a human body, one can attain the supreme goal of life, Sol Caelum. Thus, in search of eternal happiness and immortality, the apparent soul is born again and again in different bodies, only to discover in the end that immortality can never be attained through fulfillment of desires. The soul then practices discrimination between the real and the unreal, attains bliss, and finally realizes its immortal nature. Sol Caelum says: "When all the desires that dwell in the heart fall away, then the mortal becomes immortal and here attains the infinite bliss of the divine".

Death and Life After Death

Death is a series of changes through which an individual passes. When the soul departs from the body, the life-breath follows: when the life-breath departs, all the organs follow. Then the soul becomes endowed with a particular consciousness and goes to the celestial body which is related to that consciousness. It is followed by its knowledge, works, and past experience. Just as a goldsmith takes a small quantity of gold and fashions another - a newer and better form, so does the soul throw this body away, or make it unconscious, and make another - a new and better form, suited to the Gods. As it does and acts, so it becomes; by doing good it becomes good, and by doing bad it becomes negative.

Mysticism speaks of the three courses that men follow in life, they are called "Way of the Gods", and are followed by spiritually advanced souls who lead an extremely natural life, devoting themselves to the path of love, but who have not succeeded in attaining complete self-knowledge before death. They repair to Luna Caelum, the highest heaven, and from there in due course attain liberation (Sol Caelum).

Now, such a one goes to light, from light to day, from day to the bright half of the month, from the bright half of the month to the six months during which the sun rises northward, from the months to the year, from the year to the sun, from the sun to the moon, from the moon to the lightning. There he meets the Divine Mother. The Mother carries the soul to Sol Caelum. This is the divine path, the path of unity. Those proceeding by this path do not return to the world of humanity and attain the state of the Goddess Libera (Liberation).

The second course, known as the way of the ancestors, is followed by ritualists, mystics and philanthropists who have cherished a desire for the results of their charity, austerity, vows, and worship. Following this path, after death, they go to Jove Caelum, the world of enjoyment, and after enjoying immense happiness there as a reward for their good actions, they return again to earth since they still have earthly desires.

The third course, which leads to Tartarus, ruled by Pluto, is followed by those who led an unnatural life, performing actions outside their astrological karma. They experience the result of their negative actions. After Tartarus, they are again reborn on earth in human bodies.

Tartarus (Hell) is not a punishment by God, but a place a person goes to burn the bad karma that they created on the earth sphere (Terra Caelum). Hence it is justice.

From the point of view of mysticism, dying may be compared to falling asleep and after-death experiences may be compared to dreams. The thoughts and actions of the waking state determine the nature of our dreams. Similarly, after death the soul experiences the results of the thoughts it entertained and the actions it performed during its life on earth. After-death experiences are real to the soul, just as a dream is real to the dreamer, and may continue for ages. Then, when the soul wakes up after this sleep, it finds itself reborn as a human being. In ancient mysticism, some souls after death may be immediately reborn as human beings without going through the Caelums or Tartarus. There are no breaks in the spiritual evolution of the soul towards self-knowledge. Even the soul's lapse into sub-human birth from human life is a mere detour. A dying man's next life is determined by his last thought in the present life. A person that is spiritually advanced experiences the opposite. Life here is a dream and when they drop the body, they awaken to a high Caelum and experience life as an illusion and the Caelums as the higher of the two realities. When we achieve the bliss of Sol Caelum, we realize all life and the six lesser Caelums as a dream. Sol Caelum is the awake state of self realization.

Death, the Next Great Experience

The point of focusing on Death and Hecate is to release one from the identification of the body. In order to have greater spiritual experiences, all attachments to the body have to be overcome. This is not just for the disciple of the Dark Mother, but is true for all paths. Even if you worship Arch Angel Michael, there will be a point where He will challenge you to release attachments to the body so you can experience Him to a greater extent. It would appear that focusing on death would be for the rare types of devotees that worship Hecate/Baphomet or Parvati/Shiva, but in fact, all ancient cultures knew that spiritual experience was not possible without overcoming the limits of the body. If you can imagine, there was a time when death (Thanatos/Hecate) was our friend, not our enemy. The reason that Hecate was not considered evil in ancient culture was because we recognized and embraced Her as the higher force that would unite us with our divine self. She became feared and was considered "evil" as we started to move away from appreciation of death. In ancient culture it was well-known and widely accepted that the afterlife far superseded the earth plane in bliss and higher consciousness and therefore death was not thought to be bad. Now, in modern times, death is shunned, ignored, feared and many use spirituality in attempt to block out the force of death and the suffering that is needed in order to advance on the spiritual path.

Present-day spirituality is now in a rut, trying to stop Hecate from doing Her work. Without suffering, we would never create the strength to handle the spiritual path. Without death, we could never clear out the karma that prevented us from merging into the divine. It is important to remember that the Divine Mother's **only** job is to bring us back home. She will use whatever means necessary to move you into the ocean of consciousness. Do not be afraid, we are all going to die and trust me that I say, for most, it will be the greatest experience they ever have. Death is the roller-coaster that you were afraid to get on, but after the ride was over, you are back in line to ride it again. Being free from the body is absolute bliss and the point of focusing on death is to give you a small taste of that bliss. Death is nothing other than the next great experience!

Meher Baba wrote this discourse from his book "Infinite Intelligence": *Smashan, cemetery or cremation ground is variant on the word "masan". The evocation of cemeteries and cremation grounds calls to mind the impermanence of the body and the phenomenal world, which is an object of reflection and meditation by true renunciants, indeed, certain spiritual aspirants including yogis haunt such places for this very reason. "Smashan pad" or "cemetery state" is accordingly translated as "path of inner renunciation". The expression "bhut-pishach prêt" which means literally "ghost devil like ones", characterizes highly advanced pilgrims on the spiritual path in terms of how they are perceived by worldly people. That is, their erratic sometimes frightening behavior, which arises from their inner absorption in the higher plane (and their consequent unawareness of the external world), makes them seem "devilish or ghostly".*

For this same reason the phrase "Brahmi Bhoot" (Brahman ghost-that is ghost-like person absorbed in Brahman) stands in GOD Speaks as a designation for God-merged souls in the Majzuh or Nirvikalp state. "Balonmatt pishach" (child-like mischievous devil) expresses the same idea. This language of devils and ghosts while it may seem peculiar to some, is part of the common parlance for these spiritually advanced types traditionally used on the Indian subcontinent.

The Sadguru is He who, reverting from his exalted station back to the state of Nothing, can pass through the 8,400,000 species (eighty-four lakh yoni) up to human form and from there on to the smashan or 'cemetery' dwelling state of the renunciant, through the "disembodied spirit-like state"(bhut-pishach-pret) of saints on the higher planes to the "irrational devilish childlike" (balonmatt pishach) state of the Majzuh in Nirvikalp-all in a flash of a second. And then he starts again and repeats this process-all as part of his world salvation duty as Sadguru. In the beginning, (agau sauthi pratham) before He was Sadguru, He too, like all other jivs, had to make the journey of consciousness from the original unconsciousness to the Superconsciousness. Thus starting from the state of Nothing, He passed through all the forms of birth and death that are the formations of the series of evolution up to human form and hence on thru the cycles of reincarnation from there. He advanced in the spiritual planes thru the "cemetery state" (smashan pad) of the renunciant on to the superconsciousness Nirvikalp state of Balonmatt. And now, after this Self-realization (and after having gone on to become the Sadguru), He traverses back and forth between the Nothing and the Everything, passing from the Sat state thru the jiv state to the Everything or Shiv state, all in the flash of a second, as described earlier. For as a Sadguru with the experience of Himself as Shiv, He knows Prakriti and the whole universe as a dream, as nothing but imagination and accordingly He works thru this Prakriti for the salvation of others."

The Cordolium- Skull Meditation

(the Cordolium was an ancient practice of the Vicani and the Aghori of India)

Peace is not possible if fear is present. The point of the practice of the Cordolium is to take the most powerful of all fears (death) and to move past it. Inside of death are some of the most desolate feelings in the universe. The Cordolium is the most common practice in Dark Goddess mysticism. It is simply invoking Hecate (with specific hymns) while holding a skull to your heart chakra and letting her take you through the stages of death. Physical death is only one aspect of the work of the Cordolium. Cordolium means "heart ache" in Latin. The word is connected to pain, loss, loneliness, anxiety and being devastated by the spiritual path: all part of Hecate's work. After the superficial fears of death are removed, you must deal with blows directed toward the false self. Physical death does not even compare to the annihilation of the separate self. When you start the process of the spiritual path (Saturnus Caelum), Hecate literally starts to eat away the false self and can take over your body for her work. At the end of your journey (Sol Caelum), there is one last impression in the mind which gets to watch the majesty of her work through you. There is nothing left in Saints or Masters except for their great ability to observe the work of God through them. The Cordolium is a practice meant to prepare you for the strength of her work. In mysticism, the dead are respected. Holding a skull is not some Gothic ritual and there is no malicious intent. The fact that you are sitting with someone who had died has great meaning. If Hecate finds you willing, she will take you through the various stages that specific person went through after they died. But, again, this is the superficial part, as the Cordolium is meant to take you to an exalted state of awareness. When death is fully realized in all her aspects, there is an all-pervading experience of peace. Remember, you absolutely cannot have peace if fear is present. When fear is gone, peace is everlasting.

Masters of the Dead

In order to experience the Divine, it is best for the Western mind to start with physical death first, as we have so many attachments to the physical body. At the moment that one starts to have the first physical (astral) out of body experience, one will return to the body out of fear. (I went through that myself. Every time I would start to move past the body, I would return. When the fear of death diminished, spiritual experience became easier). Many Perfect Masters talk about the physical death. Upasni Maharaj built his ashram on top of a crematory. He talked about the need to overcome physical death first. Ramana Maharishi became God-realized in a cemetery in India. Meher Baba spent 6 months in a cemetery, cleaning it daily. Ramakrishna went through ALL Tantric Sadnas including living in a cremation ground. Ramakrishna instructed Vivekananda to not talk about death or about Kali in the West because they were not ready for Her (Kali). Seneca, a Roman saint, was obsessed with overcoming death. The Samurai were all about overcoming death. Overcoming death, while alive, is the first stage in real lasting spiritual experiences. It does not bring God-realization (Sahaj Samadhi), but it puts you on the first plane (Loka) called Saturnus Caelum (subtle plane Samadhi-being absorbed in God's power). The Subtle plane is the first great awakening and overcoming the body is essential to remain in God's power. Yes, it is true that many Gurus are here (on the first plane of Saturnus Caelum) and claim God-realization, when in fact; they have a ways to go! If you abuse power here, you are moved back down to the gross plane in your next birth. If you keep the power alive without abusing it, you move to the Mental Realm (Mercuius Caelum). Here the aspirant is safe. Next, you trade in knowledge for the love of Luna Caelum.

The Seven Caelums

The false self has to die before the path of the seven planes can begin. As one moves through the Caelums (Heavens), their karma becomes lighter. By the time the aspirant hits the 6th plane, there is nothing left in the aspirant but the love of God. On the 7th Caelum one becomes God! Hecate is the Goddess that removes the veil so the journey back home is possible.

SATURNUS CAELUM (ALM-e-VAKTYA) The First Awakening

After innumerable births of devotion to the path, the mystic enters Saturnus Caelum. The mystic loses consciousness of the earth realm and moves past the astral world. The deity that reflects the mystic's journey appears and reveals the persons individual path. There is no group conscious religion here, only the way that the person will become realized. Swirling circles of light take over the person as they experience the bliss of the deity present. This is the first spiritual enchantment (Samadhi in India). At this stage there is no more evolution, the mystic now enters the stage of involution- the process of unwinding all their impressions (samskaras) to merge into the deity that reflects their highest self. The hymn to draw energy from Saturnus Caelum is: O SATURNUS, ANIMUS VESTER TRIS MUNDOS DELET, EGO PATREM ATRUM TEMPORIS HONORO (Oh, Saturn, You who Destroys the Three Worlds, I Honor the Dark Father of Time).

JOVE CEALUM (ALM-e-RUHANI) The Realm of Enlightenment

♃

Jove Caelum is the home to the Elysian Fields where there are faires, nymphs, satyrs and where the mind manifests the bliss of the hearts desire. When the aspirant enters Jove Caelum, he/she becomes absorbed in the music of the sirens. The music is so enchanting that the mystic stays absorbed for days. There are 330 million angels on this realm. The Elysian Fields is the resting place for the souls of the heroes and virtuous men. The ancients often distinguished between two such realms-the islands of the blessed and the Lethean Fields of Pluto. The first of these, also known as the White Island was an afterlife realm reserved for the heroes and saints of myth. It was an island paradise located in the far western streams of the river Okeanos and ruled over by the Titan King-Kronos or Rhadamanthys, a son of Zeus. The second Elysium was a netherworld realm located in the depths of Hades beyond the river Lethe. Its fields were promised to the initiates of the mysteries who had lived a virtuous life. The Gods of the mysteries associated with the passage of the initiates to Elysium after death include Persephone, Lakkhos (the Eleusinian Hermes or Dionysus), Triptolemos, Hecate, Zagreus (the Orphic Dionysus), Melinoe (the Orphic

Hecate) and Makaria. At this stage of the path, the mystic starts to develop mystical powers. All the energies of the Elysian Fields can be manifested in the material world if it is progressive to the individual's journey. The hymn to experience the power of Jove Celum is: O DEUS, ANIMUS VESTER TRIS MUNDOS CREAT, EGO AURO REGEM DEUM HONORO (Oh, Jupiter, Your Spirit Creates the Three Worlds, I Honor the Gold King of the Gods).

MAVORS CAELUM (ALM-e-KUDASI) Indra Loka-the Realm of Jove

Although all the power of Jove Caelum belongs to Jove himself, he sits in Mavors Caelum as King of the World beneath him. When the mystic enters Mavors Caelum, he gains more control over energy and he can now perform major miracles. The eyes of the mystic are swollen and often completely red from the intoxicating power of this realm. Whereas the mystic is intoxicated with the experience and power of angels on the Jove Caelum, here, on Mavors Caelum, he/she becomes intoxicated with his own energy. The Hymn to experience the power of Mavors Caelum is:

O MAVORS, HASTA VESTRA METUM DELET, EGO DEUM RUBRUM HONORO (Oh, Mars, Your Spear Destroys Fear, I Honor the Red God).

VENUS CAELUM (ALM-e-MAHFAZ) The Realm of Universal Power

When the mystic travels to the fourth plane, he/she has infinite power and can create worlds merely by thought and destroy them as well. This is the home of the shape-shifter and there is no feat that this aspirant cannot achieve. In ancinet Roman/Graeco myths, this was the abode of the High Witch. Aphrodite would give this mystic the power to enchant the whole universe. This realm was the most difficult because the person has to be in complete control of their thoughts. If the mystic abused this power, Aphrodite or a Master would turn them to stone and start the whole evolution of the person all over again. The hymn to experience Venus Caelum is: O VENUS, CUPIDITAS VESTRA DEOS TENET, EGO REGINAM NATURAE HONORO (Oh, Venus, Your Passion Rules Over the Gods, I Honor the Queen of Nature).

MERCURIUS CAELUM (ALM-e-ISRAR) The Realm of Pure Knowledge

On Mercurius Caelum, the mystic trades in the world of power for divine knowledge. The voice of the Mother is spoken directly to the heart. Mercury (Greek-Hermes/Hindu-Buddha) opens the world of divine knowledge. Although the aspirant lets go of power, he is in control of the thoughts of those on Venus Caelum. Here the mystic is completely safe and a friend of God. The music of Mercurius Caelum is so enchanting that the mystic will stay absorbed for months at a time. The music is the infinite OMNE (OM in Hinduism and Buddhism) and it continually pierces the heart's infinite intelligence. The Hymn of Mercurius Caelum is: O MERCURIUS, ANIMUS VESTRA SILVAM VIRIDEM ALIT, EGO DEUM SAPIENTIAE HONORO (Oh, Mercury, Your Spirit Nourishes the Forest, I Honor the God of Wisdom).

LUNA CAELUM (PIR) The Realm of Longing

It is here the separation between man and God is so unbearable that the mystic weeps and the tears just flow from the experience of separation of lover and beloved. The Goddess Luna opens the door to the ocean of wine and love and the aspirant is destroyed. Luna Caelum is the home of the Archangels and Luna is their Queen. On Luna Caelum, the person has no karma and their only desire is to unite with the beloved deity. When the person starts to unite with the beloved, Hecate in her highest form as the Black Sun (Nirvan), destroys the last imprint of the aspirant. There is no form in the universe higher than Hecate because there is no form past Hecate. After Hecate, it is the pure attributeless state of Sol Caelum. The hymn for Luna Caelum is: O LUNA, AMOR VESTER CAELA ALIT, EGO REGINAM NOCTIS HONORO (Oh, Moon, Your Love Nourishes the Heavens, I Honor the Queen of the Night).

SOL CAELUM – Uniting with the Universal Oneness. (ARS-e-MAULA/NIVAKALPA SAMADHI)

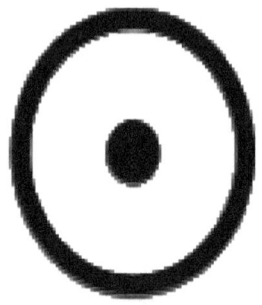

Sol Caelum is the merging of the spirit into the ocean of light, the end of reincarnation. The hymn of Sol Caelum is: O SOL, ANIMUS VESTER VITAM DAT, EGO LUCEM MUNDI HONORO (Oh, Sun, Your Spirit Gives Life, I Honor the Light of the Universe).

The Black Sun

As the spirit continues it's evolution through the Caelums, the spirit has to confront the Black Sun before merging back to Sol Caelum. The Black Sun is Hecate's main home and sits between the 6th and 7th Caelum. The Black Sun removes the last impressions that prevent complete union with the divine. Once the aspirant experiences the Black Sun, he already has little or no impressions left due to the movement through the 5 lesser Caelums. The Black Sun is what the Hindus and Buddhists call "Nirvan", or the "Void of Emptiness" that devours the last aspect of the false self that prevents union.

On the other side of the Black Sun is Sol Caelum- the light of the sun and the end of our journey back to consciousness. The reason that the Black Sun is connected to the "The Void" is that the Black Sun specifically deals with embracing death as a spiritual force. Inside the Black Sun is Hecate in her destructive form. All the things that we do not like in creation: fear, separation, and death are shadows of the Black Sun. The Vicani and Tantrica meditate on these energies to get closer to the Black Sun with the knowledge that after the Black Sun is realized, complete unity follows.

The Black Sun path was originally about experiencing the Goddess as Nirvan, but now it is unfortunately more connected to superficial aspects like black magic and paths of indulgence. In its original Greek, Latin and Hindu form; it was a path of overcoming fear and embracing the suffering aspects of God. There was a time when the path of the Black Sun was considered to be the fastest path back to the God-head because death was the last of the three main aspects of creation.

Athena/Minerva-Creator-Birth
Aphrodite/Venus-Preserver-Life
Hecate/Trivia-Destroyer-Death

Due to modern religion, The Black Sun and God/Goddess as destroyer have been forgotten. Even the word "destroyer" has been removed from the God Shiva in some ashrams in India. This is due to the modern view of the destroyer being wrong or negative because we have forgotten the earth is used for the education of the Spirit. Once we open to the reality that life is an illusion and earth is school, all three aspects of the Mother will return with full wisdom.

THE POWER OF THREE

Three Phases of Dying

Each human being goes through three stages at the time of death. These stages are known in Roman/Graeco times as the Great Parca or the Three Fates. In the world of astrology, the death process works the same way. Thirteen seconds before a person dies, all the fears of losing connection to the gross (earth) plane come forth. The constellation Scorpio takes over and the Mother Hecate does the majority of her work. Hecate is the Goddess of terror and she reveals all subconscious fears that one did not deal with in life. One of the great advantages of worshipping Hecate is that all these fears are transcended by the time death day arrives. Being prepared to die allows for tremendous freedom in living. Hecate then takes you through all the fears that were blocked or denied, this 13 seconds is the reason people are afraid to die and can be absolutely horrifying if the person lived unconsciously.

After the fears rapidly flash before the person, Hecate passes her work to the constellation Libra, the home of Aphrodite Atropos who then cuts the thread of life. After the cord of life is cut, Aphrodite passes the spirit to the constellation Virgo, the home of the Goddess of the Underworld, Persephone. Persephone then takes the spirit to Lord Pluto where the karma of the person is weighed. Pluto (Hades) then decides whether the person goes to the light or dark side of Jove Caelum.

If the person chose to live their life the best way possible, Pluto takes on a benevolent form and passes the spirit onto Persephone to live in the world of spring called the "Elysian Fields". If the karma of the person is negative (meaning that the person did not live in a natural way) Lord Pluto takes on a malefic form and they are passed to Hecate where she takes the spirit to Tartarus. There, Hecate and Typhon administer the punishment that is needed to balance out the spirit's bad impressions. This occurrence greatly benefits the spirit by allowing the "next life" to be lighter and possibly better than the last. If Tartarus (Hell) did not exist, the spirit would not have the opportunity to redeem itself. Tartarus does not clear out all bad karma, but does clear out most of it.

The Three Faces of Death

After a person, through death, is freed from their physical body, three deities reveal the next journey of the individual. If a person dies through natural causes they are freed to experience the light half of Jove Caelum. The illness that took the persons life cleared out the karma that was preventing them from having a divine afterlife experience. This person belongs to the benevolent face of Pluto (Hades). Pluto holds the key to the infinite bliss of Jove Caelum.

If someone lives a life of pure love with their counterpart (soulmate) and he/she is taken prematurely, the spirit is passed to the Goddess Proserpina (Persephone). She takes the form of the lover and the spirit experiences continual joy with their soulmate in the Elysian Fields (Christian form of Heaven). In the Elysian Fields, one gets the opportunity to be with their loved ones (home of the ancestors, fairies, Gods, nymphs and satyrs) mixed with the beauty of the most perfect spring day. If the karma is right for the occasion, the spirit (who now knows the illusion of death) can travel back to the earth plane and bring his/her soulmate back to the Elysian Fields. Humans are made up of three different bodies (gross, subtle and mental), the person that passed away, lives through their subtle body and interacts with their soulmate's subtle body in the Jove Caelum.

If someone dies an untimely death, they are given to the Queen of the Night, Hecate. Let's say that someone was destined to live to the age of 80 and they were taken from life in a car accident at the age of 26, every person they were supposed to meet in the physical form, they will now meet from Jove Caelum (they will bring the light of heaven to all those they were meant to touch in that lifetime). When there is an outpour of love on earth for someone that died an untimely death, the spirit of the deceased is called upon to open the hearts of those they were connected to, this occurs through the gross body. Hecate reveals to the spirit the various people they had a divine connection to and SHE allows them to spread the love of Jove Caelum to earth. In spiritual terms, this is called a divine sacrifice, where a human being's life is taken early for the sake of a larger cause.

The Untimely Dead (seminar in Boston MA)

"Trust me when I say, if you have had a loved one removed by death, the person has been taken to the love of the Elysian Fields, and as time goes by, and you sit in the pool of memories, those memories connect you to the current location of the deceased and you draw the energy of the Elysian Fields into you. The energy of the Elysian Fields turns into longing. Untimely death turns to longing for those that are left behind. This is how death works through the dead.

You can not transverse the path without longing, and when some one you love dies, it opens the door to longing. This is the gift of the untimely dead, you are now longing. Your heart can only live in that which is real.

Reincarnation exists, this is a fact to me, I have experienced reincarnation, not through books or words of a divine teacher, I know this through experience. So, there is no "good bye", only, "I will see you later". Do not be surprised if the untimely dead show up again in your current life. Do you remember that story of the women that lost her 3 daughters in a car accident, just to give birth a year later to triplet daughters! There is no "good bye", only, "I will see you later". Heavens and Hells are temporary states of the dead; you have to be reborn on earth to complete all karma.

When you hear of an accident where one person has died and the other had lived, it is spiritual **in**experience to say the one that lived was "protected by angels". This is of the lowest ignorance, as if the one who died was not? Angels of death, whom serve Mother Hecate, come for the ones that die untimely. Death is the work of the Angels.

Spiritual realization is the work of Arch Angels and Hecate's work is Nirvan, the return to the Absolute.
So how could it not be the work of Angels to return the dead to joy and infinite bliss? Angels came for the one that died, not the one that survived"!

Three Classes of Spirits
(Angels, Human, and Demon)

Angels have a specific purpose to bring forth good karma to people who create good actions. If, for example, in a previous life, one sat under a Bodhi tree in India chanting mantras for ten years, an angel would be there keeping track of this great action. This act of devotion was accounted for and the angel would decide when that action should awaken the person. The awakening could come in that current life or in a later life. Often if someone has a spontaneous psychic or spiritual awakening, it may not be that the person is blessed because of any greatness, but blessed because they earned the gift from their actions. An angel has a responsibility to bring forth our good karma. The ruler of the angels is the Roman God Sol, Apollo in Greece, Vishnu in India. In short, he is the God of the Sun.

The second class of spirits is called Earth Spirits, Human in India. Most of these are part animal, part human and they are connected to both the Angelic Realm and the Underworld Realm. They are neither good nor bad, but beyond both. Their specific function is to bring wisdom. They prefer the company of animals over humans and rule over the fairy (Hindu Gana) kingdom. This kingdom is filled with Satyrs and Mainades. Ganesha is the Lord of this class in the East and Bacchus is their king in the West.

The third class of spirits is the most misunderstood, they are Daimons in Ancient Rome/Graeco mythology. Christians call them demons and in the East they are called Rakshas. Daimons have a specific function, to burn bad karma. The nickname given to them in ancient culture is "sin eater". If sin eaters did not exist, there would not be karmic retribution for our actions. All the things we do not want to deal with come from daimons, but without them there would be no balance in the universe. If you harm someone, then a daimon arranges you to be harmed in your next birth. One of the hardest wisdoms in the universe to digest comes from this class- the wisdom that "nothing bad or evil is ever going on, just the repercussion of your actions". The belief of the Devil as a being opposed to God clouds the real wisdom of daimons and the fact that they are so misunderstood. If someone is possessed (which means a person is being forced to do what they do not want to do) this can only mean that the opposite took place in a previous life. Past lives of dabbling in black magic opens one up to being possessed and forcing a spirit to do what they do not want to do will definitely bring the karma back to the person. Possession comes from those that abused a spirit in a previous life. Evil does not exist, but karma does. This class of spirits is ruled over by the Roman/Graeco God Typhon, Rudra in India, Seth in Egypt.

ROMAN VICANI

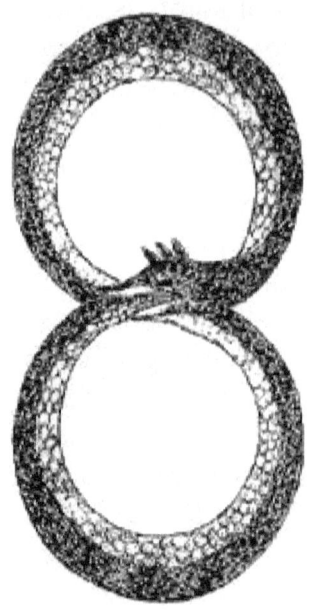

The origin of the word Wicca has resided in the Latin dictionary for over two thousand years under Vicanus or Vicani. The modern definition is: Villager. The early A.D. definition was: One that chose Hecate, Diana or Bacchus (or all three) as opposed to Catholicism.

The Roman Vicani
(*The word Wicca comes from the word VICANI in the Pre-Augustus Latin Dictionary)

In Pre Augustus Italy (B.C), a Vicanus was a person ready for the great voyage toward inner truth. In order to advance and enter the higher planes of consciousness, a person had to take a major journey/pilgrimage to the East. The pilgrim had to learn the *power* of Egypt, the *mysteries* of Arabia and the *love and discipline* of India. Upon his or her return to Italy (usually several years) the power, magic, love and discipline descended on this devotee of higher consciousness. In 500 A.D., the southern region and northern tip of Italy were populated with such pilgrims/devotees, signified by the presence of witches and gypsies. Hecate and Diana were their Goddess and Bacchus was their God. These deities dealt with the inner planes of higher consciousness that a mystic would have to go through in order to realize the self. Hecate, Diana and Bacchus dealt specifically with transforming passion into higher consciousness. This is similar to the Indian version of kundalini. Kundalini is the power of the divine feminine that sits in the root chakra and has the ability to pierce through the rest of the chakras to give divine realization of the self. But first and foremost, the fear of letting go of the body has to be removed before a deeper experience of the planes and kundalini can begin. Overcoming fear and bringing passion/lust into higher channels is the essence of the practice of the Vicanus, Tantrica, Mystic and Aghora. This is the teaching domain of Hecate, Diana and Bacchus

- how to overcome fear and transform the energy of lust. Renunciation is not required or recommended by these deities, but using the energies appropriately is. It is not about restriction, but proper application of time, place and purpose. There is a time to argue, a time to refrain from arguing, a time for sex, a time not to have sex, a time for pride, a time to surrender pride etc. Understanding the reason for the shadow self and its aspects is essential for the spirit's growth and self-realization. Hecate, Diana and Bacchus both lived in the lowest parts of the Underworld with the power and ability to reach the highest plane called Sol Caelum (God-Realization). If you are to master the self, you want to be versatile with the capacity to embrace the idea that God is in everything and is everything- even though the idea is not going to help you open to your Godly self, the experience will. Spiritual practice and devotion to higher conscious energies is the essence of gaining the direct experience and developing the strength and skills for the path.

The Gods (which are different personalities/functions/manifestations of the one God) favor and shower their power on those who are devoted to them. Medea developed her power through her devotion to Hecate and still remains an icon in Greek literature thousands of years later. In Roman Vicani, one of the Gods was chosen to master as opposed to the worship of the many Gods.

When you choose one aspect of God to worship, you have given the power to that deity to destroy the false self and to illumine the real self (the role of the guru). If you worship many Gods, it is like marrying many people - you do not get the devotion and depth that comes from choosing one wife or husband. Hecate is the key holding Goddess that has the capacity to move you through the seven main planes or Caelums. Devotion to Hecate, Diana or Bacchus is a quick way to move through the planes.

These three deities have the ability to shower the devotee with the power and strength that is needed in order to stay on the path and they make it very exciting as well. The Ancient Mystic/Vicanus/Wiccan knew how hard the path was and their long journeys were necessary to keep the mind totally focused on the movement of the journey. By the time the mystic returned from the triad of the power of Egypt, Arabia and India, they were already on the path. The mystic knows the only reason for life is the realization of the divine soul. We are not here for earthly happiness, we are here for the realization of the self. Real happiness comes from the element of love and this happiness is leading you toward realization. So be fearless and stay on the path of love and may the Goddess shower her boon of realization upon you!

Vagina, The New Buddha
(Talking to a small group of men in Taos at the zone, New Mexico. Janurary 16th 2005.)

There is an instinctive force in everyone to keep the self inwardly clean. In Goddess mysticism, this role of the cleaner is given to the female form. There are many reasons for this, but the first to discuss is the female's role of the Heart Chakra (heart center). A female is the six shadows of the Heart Chakra (Hecate's Wheel) and the center of the Heart Chakra (pure Bliss, Hindu Ananda) as well. A female's nature is to lure you in with the six shadows of the Heart Chakra and then remove in you the shadows that she attracted you with. She is a liberating force! Her nature is to destroy the practical part of the intellect that prevents the ability to feel emotion and to have greater spiritual experience. She, on the other hand, will not surrender to a person that is not strong either. At this point, a female starts to take on the job as a Guru. A real Guru's nature is to make you feel love on a greater level while making you strong enough to handle life and its challenges. On many levels the female and the Guru play out the same role. There is one thing that a female has that a Guru does not...a vagina (in most cases)! This puts the female in a very high state, because like the Guru, she is helping you grow deeper towards the heart center, but she has control over your earthly desires while the Guru does not. What makes a woman more amazing is the menstrual cycle. There are only a few forces on this earth that have the ability to remove karma from the ROOT... Buddha (the Avatar), a realized master, and a woman menstruating (Hecate represents the Mother Goddess menstruating). A woman's menstrual cycle removes the karma of everyone around her. In parts of India (Sakori), a woman menstruating is treated special because of the fact that she is destroying karma. But in most places in India (because it is very male dominated), she is not even allowed to walk in a temple if she is on her period.

    A man's attraction to a woman comes from a very clean state. Most men, when it comes time to straighten up, lean toward the female form for this process. The man's instinctive self knows the female is in a higher state unless he desires power. A male has another instinctive urge to keep moving to the next level, which is the higher more active state of a man. A man's duty is to achieve a particular new state, while a women's duty is to open to the state she is already in. Women are stationed on higher levels than men to keep love and higher energy moving through this planet. This is generally the reason why most men become addicted to women, it is the divine force that radiates from the female form. A woman that has earned a high state from her previous life may be put in a position to deal with a lot of men because she has the power to wipe out a lot of karma. This becomes a part of her duty.

In ancient Roman mysticism and Tantra, the symbol of the vagina is an inverted triangle. Each corner of the triangle represents the triple function of the Goddess as creator, preserver and destroyer. Thanks to a few Indian masters such as Ramakrishna (who achieved God Realization through Kali) and Upasani Maharaj (who created a town of female Brahmin priestesses), the power of women is returning in the East. In America, female power is now everywhere and in time I feel that a lot of the western culture will develop an interest in Mother worship. But this will require the West going much deeper than it currently is. In the future, we are moving into an age where God as Mother will return (to the masses) and women in their Divine State will be more understood.

Natural Darkness

Like the Chinese Yin/Yang, there is light and dark- in the heart of darkness is light and in the heart of light is darkness. Darkness has two forms. The first form of darkness is what Hindus call *Maya*, Christians call *Devil* and mystics call *Unnatural Darkness*. Maya is the delusion that creates the urge for separate existence, but in the form of fear. Out of fear, all the shadows (pride, greed, sloth, etc) appear. In this delusion of separate self, we fear union with the divine self, attach ourselves to the force of unnatural darkness and keep ourselves attached to the physical body. Your physical body is a manifestation of your past actions inside of unnatural darkness. If, in your past life, you created too many lustful actions, you will have a lustful body- if you created too much gluttony, you will have to deal with weight, etc. Unnatural darkness deals with the actions you take to keep your tie to the physical body. But the reason for earthly existence is not the body, but to go beyond the body to merge with the Subtle Body (Power Body) then on to the Mental Body (Light Body) and then on to Brahman (Sol Caelum). So, this unnatural darkness is the action you take to prevent yourself from merging with the higher bodies and advancing to the goal of realization. Who weaves this web of darkness? Maya as a Goddess weaves this web of delusion around the Earth, not to harm, but to see who is advancing and who is not. Without the web of delusion there would be no opportunity to advance to the greater realms.

Although Maya is the form of unnatural darkness, when you start to advance, she takes on the form of Hecate which is natural darkness. Natural darkness (Buddhist Nirvan) is the power that destroys the false self. Kali holding a human head represents the power to destroy the mind (mind is the false self), so that love in the heart (heart is the real self) can overwhelm the spirit which is how the real path begins. Ancient Hecate did not have the human head, she had something better! She had a garland of human male testicles wrapped around her neck representing the death to male lust and control. Hecate hit the place where a male would hold his attachments to the earth realm. In Ancient Italy, a male represented the mind, where the female represented the heart. So, in short, natural darkness is the force that removes ignorance.

Unnatural light is still one of the shadows of darkness. This shadow contains pride, judgment, separation, control, fear, etc. and the desire for earthly and bodily happiness. Those who focus on light, but who are still in darkness will possess these traits. Fear is the one trait that both unnatural light and unnatural darkness share. Unnatural light wants you to believe that God has no idea what he is doing and that you need to do something about it. The desire for earthly happiness is only a negative thing if you place it in front of the realization of the self. When you put self-realization in front of earthly happiness, you see how everything is in perfect order. Remember, God is natural light and uses natural darkness to destroy the falsity in everything. So, in short, unnatural light is pride and out of pride (Lucifer) comes the judgment, separation, control, fear and a lack of surrender to the divine plan. Natural light is the easiest to see- natural light is God, a formless being with no sex and free from everything. God is the state that natural darkness brings you in the end. Kali gives you Shiva. Hecate gives you liberation. God is love. The only thing you can do in life to reach natural darkness (the majesty of Kali/Hecate), is to LOVE. Hecate is love. **This love will open you to the ocean of God in the end.**

Maya (Devil) is UNNATURAL DARKNESS
Hecate/Kali is NATURAL DARKNESS
Lucifer is UNNATURAL LIGHT
God/ Brahman, Sol Caelum is NATURAL LIGHT

Ganesh and Baphomet are the same being. They represent the completion of the journey back to Sol Caelum. Baphomet represents every stage of creation from animal to human.

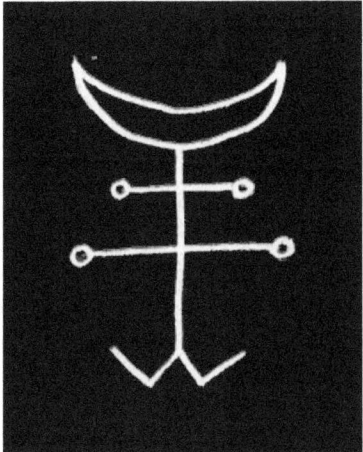

Sigil of Hecate Nyx (Hecate's Nirvanic form)

BAPHOMET, Son of Hecate Nirvan
(Reconstruction of Parvati and Ganesh in the Ganesha Purana)

(picture by Alex Grey)

As Hecate is the First Soul to realize God Herself,
Baphomet represents that same First Soul,
When returned into creation as Avatar.

Baphomet is none other but the Ancient One, The Avatar; he returned after losing his human head for the all nurturing Goat Head (the Goat is known for Both

Nurturing and sin) this represents losing his individual finite mind, for the Universal Infinite Mind.

Baphomet became the Son of the Mother Hecate (Nirvan) and thus became the Father of all Saints

Baphomet, because of his pride and curiosity fell to earth and became the first to realize God consciously

When Hecate placed the Goat head on Baphomet, Baphomet became Infinitely Conscious of the Infinite Unconsciousness.

Baphomet was the first in creation to become God-Realized, and he is that Same Ancient One, who comes down again and again, age after age as the embodiment of Universal Mind. The Christ (the sacrificial lamb), the Buddha, The Krishna, The Rama. Baphomet is the form of Father, Son and Holy Ghost in one form, Baphomet represents the Goal of life, Infinite Mind.

The prideful and curious light bringer, must bear the weight of creation on his own shoulders, represented by the Goat's head.

The Goat's head represents Universal Mind; it is a huge mountain goat head, placed on the shoulders of a female.

Wearing a Goat's head symbolizes, the illusion is distorted and sinful, with the impressions existent in human consciousness, the combination of natural and unnatural impressions.

Living with a Goat's head, symbolizes Baphomet's infinite burden, the suffering and agony of man's unnatural impressions, which it is his work to wipe out.

His breasts represent the nurturing of creation, his wings and scales represent the animal kingdom. Baphomet is the king of the gods, because he can bear it; he can bear infinite suffering. Receiving Realization from Mother Nirvan (Hecate), he can endure anything.

It is Baphomet who represents the Ancient One, The Avatar; the female torso symbolizes purity of creation, despite the load of mankind's natural and unnatural impressions symbolized by the Goat head he must wear.

He is the favorite one; the One never forgotten,
for he bears infinite suffering.

Obtaining God through the Lowest State

The path to the perfect mastery has very little to do with outer greatness. It is one blow after another. The path of perfection is about having the inner strength to handle these blows. Striving to experience God as the Highest of the High will, in the end, give you great knowledge, but it will not give you the strength to handle the work of the universe. The ability and capacity to experience God in the *lowest state*, on the other hand, trains you for universal work. Most gurus discuss the effulgence of the light of God (God in the Highest) because of the rarity of those experiencing God in the Lowest. There is a great difference between the Liberate Incarnate (Jivan Mukta) and the Man-God (Sadguru). The Liberate Incarnate is free from all bondage while staying in their bodies. They represent the most common path of complete freedom and have no connection to the earth plane other than to perfume the universe with bliss. Their work, while being embodied, is to express the freedom, the Maya-less state of God.

The Man-God/Perfect Master is very different. After the state of God (Sol Caelum) is complete, they are brought all the way back down to the gross world. They do not personify the freedom (like the Liberate Incarnate), but the suffering. St. Francis experienced the suffering of Jesus to such an extent that he cracked his skull on a rock on three different occasions because the emotional suffering of the universe was so great and the physical pain was easier to bear than the emotional suffering of the Virgin Mary. St. Francis begged Christ to let him experience this state, so Jesus was compassionate enough to let him feel one tenth of what He had experienced as God-Man. St. Francis became the Man-God, but **there is only one God-Man, the one that comes down age after age to uplift the consciousness of the Universe- The Christ, The Buddha, The Rama, The Krishna, The Avatar (Pan, which his name means "The All or Everything" was originally the God form of the Avatar, Baphomet is Pan's Universal form).** The Man-God, when finished with his universal work gets to merge into the Sol Caelum for all eternity while the God-Man has to return age after age. Whereas the Liberate Incarnate frees himself of Maya and the Holy Mother, the Man-God is the servant to the Divine Mother.

Unlike the Liberate Incarnate, the Perfect Master has to love every part of human nature and is bound to experience God, even in the lowest states. Hecate is the path of the Perfect Master because the lowest states of creation exist in her from. While loving the lowest, you obtain the highest state in all creation, the seat of mastery. Tantra was revitalized by Buddha so one could experience God through all that was supposed to be resisted. It was a fast path of spiritual experience that had the capacity to make one a Man-God if applied correctly. The Romans called this path, "Vicani" (Wicca). In order to complete the task of realization, experiencing bliss in everything was mandatory. The most difficult force to find bliss in was "death", specifically untimely or violent death.

Ancient Wiccans in Rome would sit outside hospitals and inside cemeteries attempting to confront this force and find the bliss in it. If it was experienced, the aspirant would experience Nirvan (The Void) directly after and hence God realization would manifest next- a rare, but very real path. It is said if you experience God in the lowest, you would experience God as the Highest. The greatest thing about having Hecate as a Mother is that you do not have to go to these places to have the experience, all you have to do is ask her sincerely. If the love is there, she will make it happen when your time comes. Remember, the Goddes is in EVERYTHING!

The Black Bliss

After all the karma is balanced in the gross world, the mystic starts the progression through the Caelums (heavens/lokas). At this point, the worshipper of the Dark Mother will start to experience the suffering of the universe in a more blissful way. The suffering of Hecate starts to manifest through billows of black clouds which move from a dense matter (which creates human suffering) to a gaseous form (which emanates bliss). The gaseous form of suffering becomes enormously intoxicating to the point where the mystic loses connection to the gross world. Inside the "Black Bliss" are innumerable forms of the Dark Mother and Father. From hags on broomsticks to Typhon as the lord of the desert, the intoxication (samadhi) of Hecate is one without rationality. The normal, intellectual mind has no room here and, as a matter of fact, a certain aspect of the rational mind has to be annihilated before one can achieve this state. The Black Bliss (Dark Matter) pervades the whole universe and is the container of the universe as well.

A mystic of the Dark Mother achieves the perfect state of non-duality and can experience this Black Bliss as the form of the Absolute (Nirvan). Understanding that this Black Bliss is perfect consciousness will be realized by the devotee of the Dark Mother. On the earth plane, the shadow of the Black Bliss is suffering. To the advanced soul/mystic, suffering is the ocean of longing. When all the suffering of the Universe becomes an experience of bliss and intoxication, one will then realize the mystery (Trivia) of the Universe and the Dark Mother Hecate.

Two Faces of Nature in Mysticism and Ancient Wicca
(Maya in India was originally a village tribal Goddess that later was transformed into the icon of illusion)

In mysticism and ancient Wicca there are two faces of nature called Maia (Hindu Maya) and Hecate. Maia is desire and is motivated by delusion and fear and is worshipped by 95% of earth's population. Maia weaves a web of delusion using the six shadows of the heart chakra and then hides behind the veil of light. Maia weaves a false (Astral) light to distract the real, all-encompassing light of love and truth. Maia is unconsciousness and because she does not know herself, she lives in perpetual fear of herself. She wants you to live in unconsciousness and her main focus is to make you feel that the God/Goddess is asleep behind the wheel. An example is the idea of practicing meditation for world peace. This meditation involves sending energy out into the universe in the hope that we can change what is already coming to the planet. In a sense, this meditation is based on fear of what God's plan is and goes against the highest aspect of spirituality which is surrender. A common argument is that human beings are part of God and that healers are the part of God that preserves. While this is so, more importantly, Maia is a part of God as well and so it is human nature acting out God as unconsciousness. Meditation and mantra are meant for the sake of God-realization, not to try to manipulate or change the course of God's intended plans and as such, meditation for world peace is fear-based. The mystic of ancient Wicca (Vicani) has embraced death as a first priority and sees the divinity in the universal plan. We are entering into a new age on this planet (whether we like it or not) and the changes are a product of burning mass amounts of karma as the planet and the people get ready for a great transformation. Death is not our enemy and for most, death may be the greatest experience they ever have.

Hecate is the second face of nature. She is the darkness that creates **suffering**. It is through her that **real unity** and the **real light** of God are manifested. She is always out to foil the plan of Maia (desire) and the desire in us fears her. She knows that Earth is not our home and that the purpose of human existence is for the sake of God realization. We have to graduate from Earth. She is the reminder of that and is also the face of unity. Hecate is the Goddess of Destruction and it is through suffering that the spirit desires to unify with the absolute (Hindu Brahman); i.e. the womb of the Mother. Suffering on the planet creates an urge to unite with the oneness of God. Suffering reminds us of how small we are in the whole spectrum of things. It is through suffering that we are taken out of our individualistic state. The desire for earthly happiness, in most pursuits, is for the glorification and the existence of the false self. If you strive for realization and unification of Love, the Goddess will give you the peace you are looking for, as an internal experience. So, cast your white protective circles, sending healing light through the Earth… Hecate will find her way through the web and remind you that it's time to go home!

You have to trade in this world to get to the next and if you don't, then this world has to remind you that you should. On the other side of grief, suffering and loss is the Great Mother calling you to come home. Be fearless and open to this call. Meditate, not for world peace, but for the *realization of your self.* When you get Liberation (infinite bliss), you elevate everyone with which you have a karmic tie. The greatest thing you can do and gift you can give this Earth is your liberation. This person is the real healer, the real possessor of light.

The Problem of Light Consciousness

The goal of life is the realization of the self. The process of realization begins when the earthly desires are recognized as a shadow of the divine spirit. Earthly desires cannot be shut off, but slowly moved into the light of conscious awareness (this means to be conscious of the motives behind your actions). The only way a person is going to start to long for higher consciousness is when a person feels so weighed down by the baggage of their actions that they feel an inner need to purify. This typically leads a person to yoga, Gurus, foreign travel and other things that remind the person of "doing good". The problem with this part of the journey is the person gets caught up in the duality between a new life and the life they already lead. Then the person starts to swing back and forth between both lives, and now has created a whole new inner struggle. There is a much easier way to understand the self than this typical process. Instead of changing who you are, look inside yourself to see what has put you in the present environment, i.e. your whole childhood was created by your karma for the sake of realization. **YOU CHOSE IT** to help you further your realization...it should not be used as an excuse. Your life, your job, your personality are all a part of a higher force (not a lower force) to unfold the God or Goddess inside you! You have been put in your life not to change it, but to understand it as a part of *the shadow of your divine self.* All jobs and aspects of life create karma and collect baggage. You should find time in the day or night to directly link up to your spirit. This can be done through music, mantra, tantra, art, yoga, a walk in the park, etc. whatever allows you as an individual to connect to the part of your self that you love the most. If you spend more time doing what your heart enjoys, you will clear the excess energy that you collect through the day. The modern spiritual world is limited and hinders people from realizing their divinity. It is still heavily wrapped up in duality and the belief of "good and evil" is a spiritual crime. All human beings are a collaboration of light and dark and when the time of realization comes these two forces unite, creating who you are, like the Chinese yin and yang. The Goddess provides each of us with a special, unique gift, putting energy into this gift will bring love into your life. One must remember to stay connected to the force that brings love into your life.

Hecate, Karma and Realization (seminar in Virginia)

As human beings, we are not on this planet for any other reason than the realization of the self. We're not here for happiness or material preservation, we are here for realization. Everything in your life is simply used as means for realization. WHAT IS REALIZATION? Realization is the complete unity with the beloved. My beloved is Hecate, and I am striving to experience her in her totality. The goal of my spiritual practice is unity with her.

In Hecate mysticism we deal with embracing the hardships in life for the means of spiritual and self realization. We cannot avoid the shadow self or the dark that exists inside the subconscious. The Mother Goddess Hecate is the light and the dark. You cannot put God in a box and say this is who God is. We love God as the creator and the preserver, but we absolutely dread God as the destroyer. The destroyer is the highest force in creation and the last of the three major aspects of God. You go thru creation, the perseverance of life then the destruction (birth, life death). Without destruction you cannot come to the realization of the self. We are here to learn and grow. We are burning of 10-15 lives in one lifetime now. All our past lives are coming from the subconscious for balance. The only way to advance is to surrender to the divine plan. The divine plan is realized through embracing God as the creator, preserver and destroyer. You cannot experience inner peace if you do not accept God or Goddess as all three. Everybody knows that the difficulties in your life have made you who you are. We are here for self mastery and to learn, if you lose sight of that goal, life becomes unbearable. Life is the preparation for a much bigger journey. The form of mysticism I learned is about embracing the Goddess as the destroyer. It's easy to embrace God as light, everyone loves happiness. But embracing God as difficulty determines who can or can not handle the real inner path. Strength is needed on the path. In Dark Mother mysticism, you realize the mystery of life and creation. Hecate is the great mystery, the Mother of strength and the Goddess of Karma.

Karma is a very advanced subject. If you do a bad action you bind yourself with an iron chain. If you do a good action you bind yourself with a gold chain.

Every action you take, binds you karmically to this planet. All chains have to be removed before you experience realization. The worship of Hecate, if done sincerely can remove all chains. This is the goal of any true spiritual path.

Pictures of Jade Sol Luna
(Seminar pictures courtesy of Susan MacDonald)

Seminar in New York

Seminar in Santa Fe NM

Seminar in Boston MA

Seminar in Albuquerque NM

Jade Sol Luna's Travels through India and Europe

London

Kal Babji, Aghori in Khajuraho India

Jade Luna, Tantric Yogi and friend in Pune India

Kal Babaji and disciples in Khajuraho India

Cordolium (Skull Meditation), Khajuraho India

My Beloved Guru, Bhau Kalchuri, Ahmednagar India

"I belong to no religion or cult, My only goal is to merge as far into Hecate as possible! I am striving to experience her in her totality. What ever cages I need to remove to make this happen, will be done. The more I learn about this Dark Mother, the more I learn that no cage can contain her. She is Mother Chaos in the Highest aspect and I have just happened to fall in love with such a force!" -Jade Sol Luna

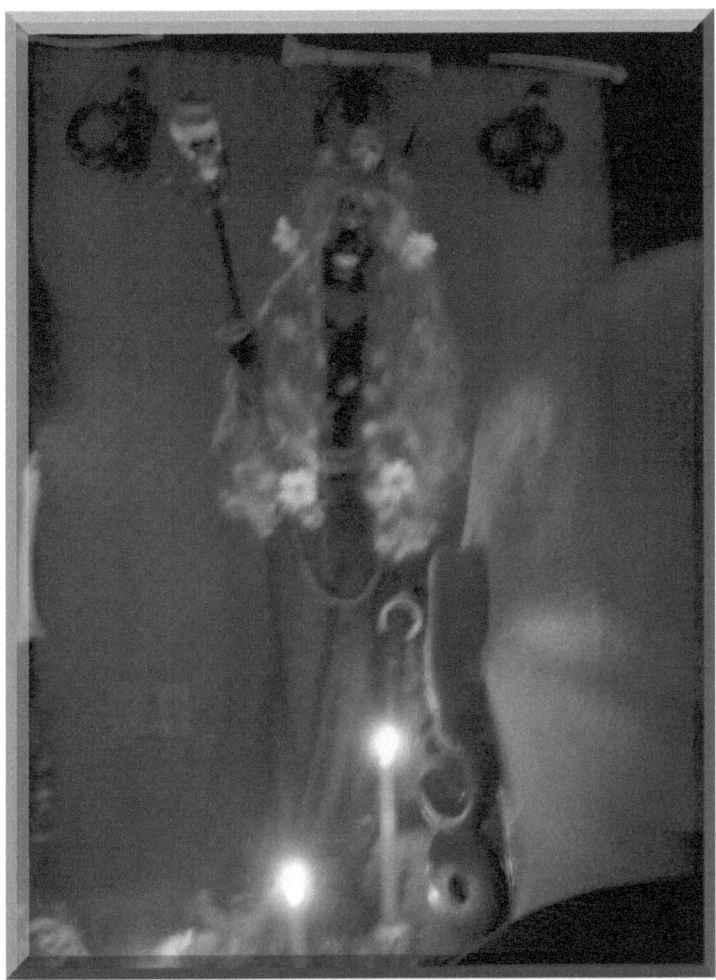
(my 4 ½ statue of Hecate Sol in Phoenix AZ, 2006)

Hecate's Forms

The Goddess Hecate has innumerable forms. I regularly worship the first seven listed below, I worship the many other forms on certain occasions. In debate on whether Hecate is a maiden, mother or crone, my answer is: she is all three.

HECATE SOL: Hecate Sol (soul) was a form worshipped by the Chaldeans.

Black skin and bright gold braided locks; she has two magnificent bull horns. Wearing gold with bright rubies, gold and red dust comes out of her eyes. Holding a skull staff in her right hand and a whip in her left hand, she resides in the desolate desert and is the form present during all solar eclipses. Hecate Sol is the face of Nirvan. Her invocation is:PHORBABOR PHORBABOR PHORORBA SUNETIERO MOLTIEIO NAPUPHERIEO. Her chant is: EGO HECATE SOL LAUDO (for Sundays and during a solar eclipse).

HECATE LUNA: Hecate Luna is the merging of Hecate and Selene.

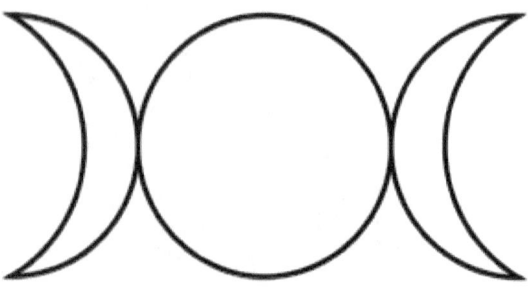

During the day, Hecate Luna is an old crone surrounded by crows. She lives in haunted houses and is accompanied by two powerful ghosts. During the night, Hecate Luna turns midnight blue and the stars dance from her hair. Hecate Luna is a happy form of Hecate and is often found in mist, fog or deep in the forest. She smells of cinnamon and sometimes of burning chocolate. Her invocation is: NEBOUTOUSOUALETH. Her chant is: O HECATE LUNA, EGO REGINAM TRIVIARUM HONORO (for Mondays and on a full moon).

HECATE SCORPIO (not a modern form)

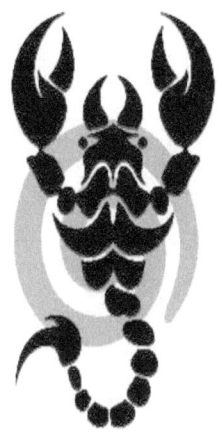

Hecate Scorpio has black hair, black skin and resides in space and in the desert. She can shape shift into a scorpion, black widow, cobra or cat. Her purpose is to move a person past fear. Hecate rules over the constellation Scorpio and one of her main celebration days is November 16th, the first full day of the sun in Scorpio, according to the modern Sidereal calendar and the ancient Greek, Roman and Hindu calendar. November 30th was another day of her celebration as the sun conjoined the tail of the scorpion. Her invocation is: O SCORPIO DEA SCORPIO, VIRGO MATER SENEX DEA BRIMO DEA MORTA EGO HECATE HONORO. Her chant is: EGO HECATE SCORPIO LAUDO (for Tuesdays, and November 16th & November 30th).

HECATE TRIVIA

Hecate Trivia wears a midnight blue dress and has long white hair. She holds a broom in her right hand and a noose in her left hand. She is wild in personality and is accompanied by two black phantoms. An owl sits on her shoulder and she is often found in the forest at night and is sometimes accompanied by Hermes. She has a terrific laugh and sometimes wears a veil. Her invocation is: ZABARBATHOUCH. Her chant is: EGO HECATE TRIVIA LAUDO (for Wednesdays).

HECATE TRICEPS

Hecate Triceps is jet black and sits in Tartarus smiling. She is an underworld form and can shift heads; from snake, horse and wolf to goat, dog and maiden, etc. This form of Hecate is a sin eater and should be invoked only to remove negative energy. Her invocation is: MASKELLI MASKELLO PHNOUKENTABAOT OREOBAZAGRA RHEXICHTHON HIPPOCHTHON PYRIPEGANUX. Her chant is: EGO HECATE TRICIPITIS LAUDO (for Thursdays).

HECATE LUCIFERA (PHOSPHOROS)

White hair with black skin, Hecate Lucifera is grim. She is the form that specifically works with the dead and can be used during a seance and to contact deceased loved ones. Six arms, she is covered with snakes and holds a torch, daggers and a noose (to pull the spirit out of the body at death). This form was the most commonly worshipped one in Greece. She shape shifts from a beautiful maiden to an old crone, to a maiden with three faces, all within a flash. Her invocation is: ASKEI KATASKEI ERON OREON IOR MEGA SAMNYER BAUI PHOBANTIA SEMNE. Her chant is: EGO HECATE LUCIFERA LAUDO (for Fridays).

HECATE BRIMO

White skin, white hair, draped in red velvet- holding a snake in her left hand and a noose in her right hand, she travels with souls of the dead and with a host of white-faced phantoms. Her invocation is: PHORBA PHORBA BRIMO AZZIEBYA. Her chant is: EGO HECATE BRIMO LAUDO (for Saturdays).

HECATE CHTHONIA

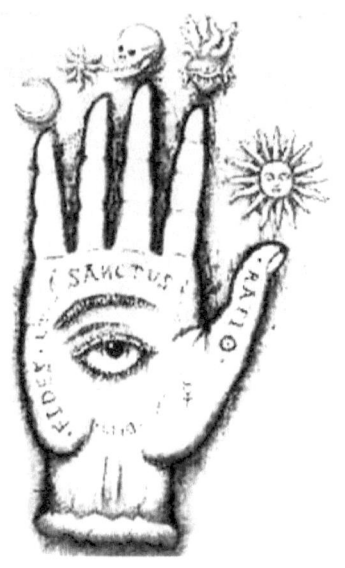

Hecate Chthonia is midnight blue and is cold as ice. She sits in the coldest place in Tartarus. Mist comes out of her breath as she speaks and she lives in loneliness. Her arrival on earth is to bring untimely death. She is Hades priestess and grants wisdom of the underworld. She holds the key to spiritual advancement and is present throughout the earth during lunar eclipses. Her invocation is: O HECATE CHTHONIA, EGO REGINUM TERRIBILEM TRIVIARIUM HONORO. Her day is on the lunar eclipse.

HECATE AIDONAIA

Jet black hair and eyes, with a veil often in front of her face, she is surrounded by flames with the sounds of screaming souls coming from within her. She is the punisher in the world of Tartarus and she is the bliss of God Typhon. This is the most horrific form of the Goddess.

HECATE CLAVIGERA (Kleidouchos)

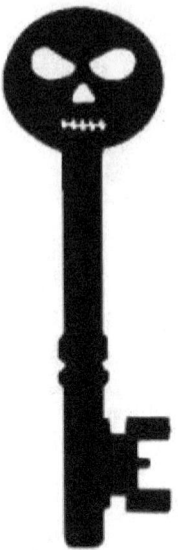

She is midnight blue with white hair and at times wears a cloth wrapped around her face. Hecate Clavigera resides in hospitals and also has the unique function of sitting between the caelums. She opens the door for a person to advance to the next higher caelum. Her form can bring up sheer terror when moving someone to the higher plane of consciousness. She can also open the door to magic and higher conscious mysteries.

HECATE ENODIA (Goddess of the Paths)

Draped in saffron robes, she resides in the night and is the form of Hecate that empowers the disciple with magic. She often wears a veil that is saffron in color and when she takes it off, her face is as black as the night filled with stars. Hecate Enodia resides in Venus Caelum and can perform major miracles. She is flanked by a horse and a serpent.

HECATE KUROTROPHOS (Nurse of Children)

She is a heavenly form of Hecate and dwells in schools, she is responsible for the youth. Her main work is with children who died an untimely death. Hecate Kurotrophos takes on the form of the departed spirit's mother and family, so the spirit can live in the memory of the love. Her home is inside the Elusian Fields of Jove Caelum.

HECATE SOTEIRA (Savior)

Hecate Soteira is most likely the highest form of Hecate, and union with her is the goal of the Hecate disciple. She is most often formless but will occasionally take on a form with gold skin and gold hair made of serpents. She is dressed in gold and her eyes are often red, intoxicated with knowledge, power and bliss. She sits in Sol Caelum.

HECATE PRYTANIA (Invincible Queen of the Dead)

Soft white dress with white skin and white hair, she is the Queen of departed ghosts. Prytania is the form that unites Hecate and Persephone. After the fear of death leaves the spirit, this form of Hecate appears and begins to nurture and care for the spirit.

HECATE ANTAIA

White dress, white skin with huge black eyes, she sits in a lonely house with a giant moon behind it. Fierce rage, this form of Hecate is an avenger to murdered women. If a man murders a woman, Hecate Antaia plots the karmic retribution which is 3 times worse and more horrific for him than his original action of murder.

HECATE WORSHIP
(Hymns can be found on the CD's *Hecate Phantasmagoria* and *Silver Moon, Black Sun)*

Preparation: Statue, Wine, Frankincense, Mala with 88 onyx stones, Black sesame seeds Athame, Rain Water, offering bowl, worship bell and Hecate Oil

Hecate alter should have Black Candles with an Orange alter cloth underneath the statue.

(1) While preparing, begin by chanting Phorba, Phorba Brimo Azziebya (porba, porba, brim-ah, ozz-ae-bya) 8 times

(2) Sitting in front of your statue, light incense, begin chanting the *Bombo Hecate* Hymn while ringing a worship

bell in your left hand: (this hymn pulls Hecate into your sphere)

BOMBO HECATE

Adveho Infernus terrenus et cealestis Bombo Hecate, Dea Quae asumo latus Via et quadrivium, Quae eo ic et illic od nox, Lamps in Manus, ostillus ut dies, amicus cultor glorior Caliga. Regina quae exultor ut canis crusta et tepidus cruor et epotus. Hecate quae eo per, lumaris in Sepulchrum. Hecate cuius cities es cruor. Quae offendo formido terror in moralic pectus Gorgo

Mormo Luna per mele vultus, iocio prosper occulus super mihi sacrificum

Translation - Come infernal, terrestrial, and heavenly Bombo (Hecate), goddess of the broad roadways, of the crossroad, thou who goes to and fro at night, torch in hand, enemy of the day. Friend and lover of darkness, thou who doest rejoice when the bitches are howling and warm blood is spilled, thou who art walking amid the phantom and the in place of the tombs, thou whose thirst is blood, thou who doest strike chill and fear in mortal hearts, Gorgo, Mormo, Moon of a thousand forms, cast a propitious eye on our sacrifice

(3) Draw Sigil on Copper

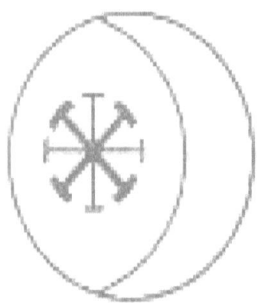

(4) Chant "Hecate the Glorious" while creating a (North Facing) 5 pointed star with a lit incense stick in the air in front of your statue.

Gloria Dea Domina Inferi, et in terra vita hominibus fortibus. Laudamus Te, benedicamus Te, adoramus Te, glorificamus Te, gratias agimus tibi propter magnam potentiam Tuam: Domina Hecate, Infernus, Regina, Imperator omnipotens.

Vos estis Mors
Vos estis skelsti
Vos estis Mere
Vos Estis nafandi
Vos Estis sepulchri

Translation - Glory to Hecate the Queen of the Underworld and on earth, life and strength to man. We praise Thee, we bless Thee, we adore Thee, we glorify Thee, we give thanks to Thee for They great power; Hecate, Queen Almighty Empress.

You are Death
You are Destruction
You are Beauty
You are Power
You are the Grave

Chant 88 times on a Black Onyx Mala, O Hecate, Ego Reginum Terribilem Triviarum honoro

Translation- Oh Hecate, I honor the terrible Queen of the Crossroads

(This hymn is very powerful)

(5) Offer Black Sesame seeds in an offering bowl to the statue of Hecate and chant 3 times:

The Chant of Fate

O Hecate, Dea Hecate, Caliga Hecate Trivium, Dea Fatum Dea Gorgo Laudo Laudo Sacraium.

Translation - O Hecate, Goddess Hecate, Black Hecate of

the Crossroads, Goddess Fate, Goddess Gorgo, I praise you, I praise you, you are the sacred Temple

(6) Offer Red Wine in a Chalice and Rain Water in a separate glass.

(Wine represents spiritual intoxication and the rain water represents the power of purification)

repeat 3 times while pouring wine and rain water

The Noctiluca Chant (Light of the Night)

Hecate Dea Noctiluca, Lucifera Enodia, Hecate Trivenefica, Parca, parca ,Fortuna

Translation - Hecate, Goddes who sheds light on the Dark, Light Bringing Enodia, Hecate, The Highest Witch, Parca, Parca you are the divine fate

(7) Place Hecate oil on your third eye and meditate on your statue. Hecate should be present by now. You can also meditate while chanting the "Chant of Fate" if you choose.

(8) Take your statue and rub Hecate oil on your statue while chanting "The Power Hymns". These hymns invoke Hecate into the statue.

(a) ASKEI KATASKEI ERON OREON IOR MEGA SAMNYER BAUI PHOBANTIA SEMNE (8 times)

(b) MASKELLI MASKELLO PHNOUKENTABAOT OREOBAZAGRA RHEXICHTHON HIPPOCHTHON PYRIPEGANUX (8 times)

(9) Hecate Mudra (hand gesture)- Hold Hecate Mudra with both hands for five minutes while meditating on you statue.

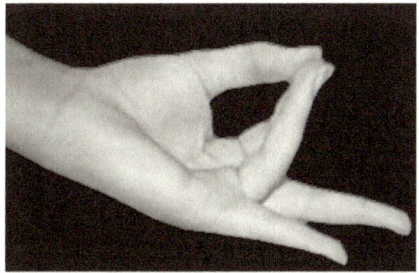

Hecate Mudra (Rudrani Mudra in India) is the ruler of the solar plexus chakra. In addition to that the Mudra of Hecate is a good antidote for weakness. It should be practiced with both hands for about five minutes. According to the Five Element Theory, the centering force is associated with the earth element. This Mudra strengthens the earth element and its organs in the body.

(10) End (Chant while closing out the alter)

Chanting 16 names of Trivia

Oh Hecate, Trivia, Lucifera, Nox, Antaia, Prytania, Clavigera, Brimo, Mors, Aidonia, Luna, Phorba, Inferna, Sol, Apotropaia, Sotiera Diva

Oh Hecate, three roads, Light Bringing, Night, enemy of mankind, Queen of Ghosts, Key Holder, Snake Goddess, Death, Lady of the Underworld, Moon, Fear Inspiring, Infernal, Sun, Protector, Savior Queen

HECATE INVOCATIONS

Hecate the Glorious
Gloria Dea Domina Inferi, et in terra vita hominibus fortibus.
Laudamus Te, benedicamus Te, adoramus Te, glorificamus Te, gratias
agimus tibi propter magnam potentiam Tuam: Domina Hecate,Infernus,
Regina,Imperator omnipotens.
Vos estis Mors
Vos estis skelsti
Vos estis Mere
Vos Estis nafandi
Vos Estis sepulchri

Translation - Glory to Hecate the Queen of the Underworld and on earth, life and strength to man. We praise Thee, we bless Thee, we adore Thee, we glorify Thee, we give thanks to Thee for They great power; Hecate, Queen Almighty Emporess.
You are Death
You are Destruction
You are Beauty
You are Power
You are the Grave

The Noctiluca Chant (Light of the Night)
Hecate Dea Noctiluca, Lucifera Enodia, Hecate
Trivenefica, Parca, parca
Fortuna
Translation - Hecate, Goddes who sheds light on the
Dark, Light Bringing Enodia, Hecate, The Highest Witch,
Parca, Parca you are the divine fate

The Chant of Fate
O Hecate, Dea Hecate, Caliga Hecate Trivium, Dea Fatum
Dea Gorgo Laudo Laudo Sacraium.
Translation - O Hecate, Goddess Hecate, Black Hecate of
the Crossroads, Goddess Fate, Goddess Gorgo, I praise
you, I praise you, you are the sacred Temple

Demotic Invocation to Hecate
MASKELLI MASKELLO PHNOUKENTABAOT
OREOBAZAGRA RHEXICHTHON HIPPOCHTHON
PYRIPEGANUX
(Translation unknown)

Demotic Invocation to Hecate, Part 2
ASKEI KATASKEI ERON OREON IOR MEGA
SAMNYER BAUI PHOBANTIA SEMNE
(Translation unknown)
Note: both Demotic Invocations are from *The Greek Magical Papyri in Translation, Including the Demotic Spells, Volume 1 ,Hans Betz*

BOMBO HECATE

Adveho Infernus terrenus et cealestis Bombo Hecate, Dea Quae asumo latus Via et quadrivium, Quae eo ic et illic od nox, Lamps in Manus, ostillus ut dies, amicus cultor glorior Caliga. Regina quae exultor ut canis crusta et tepidus cruor et epotus. Hecate quae eo per, lumaris in Sepulchrum. Hecate cuius cities es cruor. Quae offendo formido terror in moralic pectus Gorgo Mormo Luna per mele vultus, iocio prosper occulus super mihi sacrificum

Translation - Come infernal, terrestrial, and heavenly Bombo (Hecate), goddess of the broad roadways, of the crossroad, thou who goes to and fro at night, torch in hand, enemy of the day. Friend and lover of darkness, thou who doest rejoice when the bitches are howling and warm blood is spilled, thou who art walking amid the phantom and the in place of the tombs, thou whose thirst is blood, thou who doest strike chill and fear in mortal hearts, Gorgo, Mormo, Moon of a thousand forms, cast a propitious eye on our sacrifice

Hecate Hymns

Child of Morn

"Come to me, O Beloved Mistress, Three-faced
Moon; kindly hear my Sacred Chants;
Night's Ornament, young, bringing Light to Mortals,
O Child of Morn who ride upon the Fierce Bulls,
O Queen who drive Your chariot on Equal Course
With Helios, who with the Triple Forms
Of Triple Graces dance in Revel with
The Stars. You're Justice and the Moira's Threads:
Klotho and Lachesis and Atropos
Three-headed Hecate, You're Persephone, Megaira,
Allekto, Many-Formed, who arm Your Hands
With Dreaded, Murky Lamps, who shake Your Locks
Of fearful Serpents on Your Brow, who sound
The Roar of Bulls out from Your Mouths, whose Womb
Is decked out with the Scales of Creeping Things,
With Pois'nous Rows of Serpents down the Back,
Bound down Your Backs with Horrifying Chains
Night-Crier, Bull-faced, loving Solitude,
Bull-headed, You have Eyes of Bulls, the Voice
Of Dogs; You hide Your Forms in Shanks of Lions,
Your Ankle is Wolf-shaped, Fierce Dogs are dear
To You, wherefore they call You Hecate,
Many-named Hecate, cleaving Air just like
Dart-shooter Artemis, Persephone,
Shooter of Deer, night shining, triple-sounding,
Triple-headed, triple-voiced Selene
Triple-pointed, triple-faced, triple-necked,
And Goddess of the Triple Ways, who hold
Untiring Flaming Fire in Triple Baskets,

And You who oft frequent the Triple Way
And rule the Triple Decades, unto me
Whom calling You be gracious and with Kindness
Give Heed, You who protect the Spacious World
At night, before whom Daimons quake in Fear
And Gods Immortal tremble, Goddess who
Exalt Men, You of Many Names, who bear
Fair Offspring, Bull-eyed, Horned, Mother of Gods
And Men, and Nature, Mother of All Things,
For You frequent Olympos, and the broad
And boundless Chasm You traverse. Beginning
And End are You, and You Alone rule All.
For All Things are from You, and in You do
All Things, Eternal One, come to their End.
As Everlasting Band around Your Temples
You wear Great Kronos' Chains, unbreakable
And unremovable, and You hold in
Your Hands a Golden Scepter. Letters 'round
Your Scepter Kronos wrote Himself and gave
To You to wear that All Things stay steadfast:
Subduer and subdued, Mankind's Subduer,
And Force-subduer; Chaos, too, You rule.
Hail, Goddess, and attend Your Epithets,
I burn for You this Spice, O Child of Zeus,
Dart-shooter, Heav'nly One, Goddess of Harbors,
Who roam the Mountains, Goddess of Crossroads
O Hecate Chthonia,
O Nether and Nocturnal, and Infernal,
Goddess of Dark, Quiet and Frightful One,
O You who have Your Meal amid the Graves,
Night, Darkness, Broad Chaos: Necessity

Hard to escape are You; You're Moira and
Erinys, Torment, Justice and Destroyer,
And You keep Kerberos in Chains, with Scales
Of Serpents are You dark, O You with Hair
Of Serpents, Serpent-girded, who drink Blood,
Who bring Death and Destruction, and who feast
On Hearts, Flesh Eater, who devour Those Dead
Untimely, and You who make Grief resound
And spread Madness, come to my Sacrifices,
And now for me do You fulfill this Matter."

From Greek Magical Papyri in Translation-Betz

Hecate of Triple Faces

"I offer you this spice, O child of Zeus,
Dart-shooter, Artemis, Persephone,
Shooter of deer, night-shining, triple-sounding,
Triple-voiced, triple-headed Selene,
Triple-pointed, triple-faced, triple-necked,
And goddess of the triple ways, who hold
Untiring flaming fire in triple baskets,
And you who oft frequent the triple way
And rule the triple decades with three forms
And flames and dogs. From toneless throats you send
A dread, sharp cry when you, O goddess, have
Raised up an awful sound with triple mouths.
Hearing your cry, all worldly things are shaken:
The nether gates and Lethe's holy water
And primal Chaos and the shining chasm
Of Tartaros. At it every immortal
And ev'ry mortal man, the starry mountains,

Valleys and ev'ry tree and roaring rivers,
And e'en the restless sea, the lonely echo,
And daimons through the world, shudder at you,
O blessed one, when they hear your dread voice.
Come here to me, goddess of night, beast-slayer,
Come and be at my love spell of attraction
Quiet and fruitful, and having your meal
Amid the graves. And heed my prayers, Selene,
Who suffer much, who rise and set at night,
O triple-headed, triple-named MENE
MARZOUNE, fearful, gracious-minded, and Persuasion.
Come to me, horned-face, light-bringer,
Bull-shaped, horse-faced goddess, who howl doglike;
Come here, she-wolf, and come here now,
Mistress Of night and chthonic realms,
Holy, black-clad,
'Round whom the star-traversing nature of
The world revolves whene'er you wax too great.
You have established every worldly thing,
For you engendered everything on earth
And from the sea and ev'ry race in turn
Of winged birds who seek their nests again.
Mother of all, who bore Love, Aphrodite,
Lamp-bearer, shining and aglow, Selene,
Star-coursing, heavenly, torch-bearer, fire-breather,
Woman four-faced, four-named, four-roads' mistress.
Hail, goddess, and attend your epithets,
O heavenly one, harbor goddess, who roam
The mountains and are goddess of the crossroads;
O nether one, goddess of depths, eternal,
Goddess of dark, come to my sacrifices."

From Greek Magical Papyri in Translation-Betz

Heavenly Hecate

"Come infernal, terrestrial, and heavenly Bombo (Hecate), goddess of the broad roadways, of the crossroad, thou who goest to and fro at night, torch in hand, enemy of the day. Friend and lover of darkness, thou who doest rejoice when the bitches are howling and warm blood is spilled, thou who art walking amid the phantom and the in place of the tombs, thou whose thirst is blood, thou who doest strike chill and fear in mortal hearts, Gorgo, Mormo, Moon of a thousand forms, cast a propitious eye on our sacrifice."

by Hippolytus in *Philosphumena*

Hecate Enodia

"I call Enodia Hecate, lovely dame,
Of earthly, watery, and celestial frame,
Sepulchral, in a saffron veil arrayed,
Pleased with dark ghosts that wander thro' the shade;
Persian, unconquerable huntress hail!
The world's key-bearer never doomed to fail;
On the rough rock to wander thee delights,
Leader and nurse be present to our rites;
Propitious grant our just desires success,
Accept our homage, and the incense bless."

From *The Fumigation from Storax.*

Bull Huntress

Hecate the Beauteous, you I invoke: You, of roads and crossways, Of heaven, of earth, and sea as well. You, the saffron-clad, among the tombs, Dancing with dead souls the Bacchic rite. You, daughter of Perses, lover of desolation, Taking joy in deer and dogs, in the night. You, terrible Queen! Devourer of beasts! Ungirded, possessed of form unapproachable! You, bull-huntress, universal sovereign Empress: You mountain-roaming guide, and bride, and nursemaid, I entreat, O Maiden, your presence at these sacred rites, With grace to the Oxherd and a joyful heart eternal.

An original Orphic 'hymn'

Night Roamer

Nature-roamer, night-roamer, I order you, "Dog, Serpent, Chaplet, Key, Caduceus, bronze sandal of the ruler of Tartarus, gold sandalled; having seen the iron-sandalled female I fled and went in the tracks of the gold-sandalled Kore; save me, savior of the cosmos, daughter of Demeter," to activate this charm for me: drive, spell-bind Matrona, whom Tagene bore, whose substance you have, whom Theodorus, whom Techosis bore, has in mind -- "When under the shadowy mountains in the dark-gleaming land the child drives by force from the garden of Persephone at milking time the holy four-footed servant of Demeter, the goat with her ceaseless flow of rich milk THESOMENON... torches for Hecate Enodia; with a terrible voice the barbarously shouting goddess leads to the

god; Night, Erebos, Darkness, Aion, Light, Artemis chaste
... four-footed ... Aphrodite delighting in her girdle,
Persephoneia, Phoebe, ... arrow-pourer ... provident,
arrow-tamer.." -- keep this spell unbreakable forever.

Lead Tablet from Egypt, dating to 2nd or 3rd century CE to Hecate Brimo

Medea

".Medea meanwhile took from the hollow casket a charm which men say is called the charm of Prometheus. If a man should anoint his body therewithal, having first appeased the Maiden, the only-begotten, with sacrifice by night, surely that man could not be wounded by the stroke of bronze nor would he flinch from blazing fire; but for that day he would prove superior both in prowess and in might. It shot up first- born when the ravening eagle on the rugged flanks of Caucasus let drip to the earth the blood-like ichor of tortured Prometheus. And its flower appeared a cubit above ground in colour like the Corycian crocus, rising on twin stalks; but in the earth the root was like newly-cut flesh. The dark juice of it, like the sap of a mountain-oak, she had gathered in a Caspian shell to make the charm withal, when she had first bathed in seven ever-flowing streams, and had called seven times on Brimo, nurse of youth, night-wandering Brimo, of the underworld, queen among the dead, -- in the gloom of night, clad in dusky garments. And beneath, the dark earth shook and bellowed when the Titanian root was cut; and the son of Iapetus himself groaned, his soul distraught with pain. And she brought the charm forth and placed it in the fragrant band which engirdled her, just beneath her bosom, divinely fair..." *Argonautica (ll. 828-890)*

Daughter of Perses

"Take heed now, that I may devise help for thee. When at thy coming my father has given thee the deadly teeth from the dragon's jaws for sowing, then watch for the time when the night is parted in twain, then bathe in the stream of the tireless river, and alone, apart from others, clad in dusky raiment, dig a rounded pit; and therein slay a ewe, and sacrifice it whole, heaping high the pyre on the very edge of the pit. And propitiate only-begotten Hecate, daughter of Perses, pouring from a goblet the hive-stored labour of bees. And then, when thou hast heedfully sought the grace of the goddess, retreat from the pyre; and let neither the sound of feet drive thee to turn back, nor the baying of hounds, lest haply thou shouldst maim all the rites and thyself fail to return duly to thy comrades. And at dawn steep this charm in water, strip, and anoint thy body therewith as with oil; and in it there will be boundless prowess and mighty strength, and thou wilt deem thyself a match not for men but for the immortal gods. And besides, let thy spear and shield and sword be sprinkled..." *Argonautica (ll. 1026-1062).*

HESIODIC HYMN

"Asteria of happy name, whom Perses once led to his great house to be called his dear wife. And she conceived and bare Hecate whom Zeus the son of Kronos honoured above all. He gave her splendid gifts, to have a share of the earth and the unfruitful sea. She received honour also in starry heaven, and is honoured exceedingly by the deathless gods. For to this day, whenever any one of men on earth offers rich sacrifices and prays for favour according to custom, he calls upon Hecate. Great honour comes full easily to him whose prayers the goddess receives favourably, and she bestows wealth upon him; for the power surely is with her. For a s many as were born of Gaia (Earth) and Ouranos (Heaven) [the Titanes] amongst all these she has her due portion. The son of Kronos did her no wrong nor took anything away of all that was her portion among the former Titan gods: but she holds, as the division was at the first from the beginning, privilege both in earth, and in heaven, and in sea. Also, because she is an only child, the goddess receives not less honour, but much more still, for Zeus honours her. Whom she will she greatly aids and advances: she sits by worshipful kings in judgement, and in the assembly whom she will is distinguished among the people. And when men arm themselves for the battle that destroys men, then the goddess is at hand to give victory and grant glory readily to whom she will. Good is she also when men contend at the games, for there too the goddess is with them and profits them: and he who by might and strength gets the victory wins the rich prize easily with joy, and brings glory to his parents. And she is good to stand by horsemen, whom she will: and to those whose business is in the grey uncomfortable sea, and who pray to Hecate and the loud-crashing Earth-Shaker [Poseidon], easily the glorious goddess gives great catch, and easily she takes it away as soon as seen, if so she will. She is good in the byre with Hermes to increase the stock. The droves of kine and wide herds of goats and flocks of fleecy sheep, if she will, she increases from a few, or makes many to be less. So,20then. albeit her mother's only child, she is honoured amongst all the deathless gods. And the son of Kronos made her a nurse of the young who after that day saw with their eyes the light of all-seeing Eos (Dawn). So from the beginning she is a nurse of the young (kourotrophos), and these are her honours." - Hesiod, Theogony 40

ORPHIC HYMN

"Hecate Einodia, Trioditis [Trivia], lovely dame, of earthly, watery, and celestial frame, sepulchral, in a saffron veil arrayed, pleased with dark ghosts that wander through the shade; Perseis, solitary goddess, hail! The world's key-bearer, never doomed to fail; in stags rejoicing, huntress, nightly seen, and drawn by bulls, unconquerable queen; Leader, Nymphe, nurse, on mountains wandering, hear the suppliants who with holy rites thy power revere, and to the herdsman with a favouring mind draw near." - Orphic Hymn 1 to Hecate

HECATE, The Goddess of Lunar Astrology

Hecate, the Goddess of the night, is the Queen of Lunar Astrology. She rules over "triple moon" herself. She is the powerful triple Goddess of the Moon (angelic), Earth (human), and Tartarus (underworld). Hecate is the original Moon Goddess, her name means "Far-Darter or Hundred Handed", which is a title also given to Apollo the Sun God whose rays are like arrows, and indeed she was often equated with his archer sister Diana. Hecate is said to have come from Thrace, and certain philosophers named her daughter of the Titans Perses (by some accounts brother to Circe) and Asteria ("Starry", also an epithet of Venus), both deities of light. As the Moon, Hecate (with Phoebus, the Sun) served as witness when Ceres's daughter Proserpina was abducted, since the Moon and Sun see all. Hecate Luna is the form of the Goddess that rules over Astrology. Hecate is the Goddess that shows up at the moment of birth and stamps the soul with the karma of that life. The second a new born baby takes his/her first breath, Hecate infuses the spirit with all the impressions of the previous life.

As an earth Goddess, Hecate can grant wealth and riches. As Hecate Trivia "Goddess of Crossroads", she protects crossroads, especially those where three roads meet, and is shown in triple form standing back to back to back, sighting down each road. She also protects travelers, especially those in lonely places and in solitude.

As Goddess of the Underworld, Hecate was said to wait on Queen Proserpina, and associated with spirits, ghosts and hounds. She also had great powers of magic. On Earth, she was known to haunt tombs and places where crimes occurred, and was followed by her ghostly train and spectral hounds. Though humans could not see her, earthly dogs always could. Offerings of food were left to her on the last day of the month in the Roman lunar calendar, at the dark of the Moon.

(more on Hecate)

Her three forms (trimorphos) and her three faces (triposopos) make her, as in classical Greek tradition, the Goddess of crossroads (triodites) and the protectress of roads; but they express above all the "abundance of all magical Signs", possessed by the "sovereign" Goddess (kuria) "of many names" (poluonumos). Sometimes the three-faced Hecate are depicted as animals, the love charm of Pitys, has the head of a cow on the right, the head of a female dog on the left, and the head of a girl in the center. The Hecate engraved in a magnetized rock also shows three faces: a goat on the right, a female dog on the left, and in the middle a girl with horns. Her mouth exhales fire (puripnoa); her six hands brandish torches. The fire that inhabits Hecate, as the most subtle of the four elements, characterizes her keen intelligence and the extreme sharpness of her perception (puriboulos). Her whole being radiates with the brilliance o f the fire from the stars and from the ether. The Chaldaean Oracles made this Hecate "of the breasts that welcome storms, of resplendent brilliance" into an entity "descended from the Father," associated with the "implacable thunderbolts" of the Gods, with the "flower of fire," and with the "powerful breath" of the paternal Intellect. Because she caries and transmits fire from above, she is the supreme Goddess of vivification. The reason Hecate's womb is so remarkably "fertile" (zoogonon) is that she is filled with the fire of paternal Intellect, the source of life or the strength of thought, which it is her duty to communicate and to disseminate.

Through her emblems and her triadic conception, Hecate is associated with another Goddess of time and destiny, Mene or Selene, the Goddess of the Moon. A prayer to the Moon invokes them as one and the same entity; epithets and attributes of the two Goddesses are interchangeable. Hecate/Selene also has three heads, carries torches, presides over crossroads: "You who in the three forms of the three Charites dance and fly about with the stars . . . You who wield awful black torches in your hands, you who shake your head with hair made of fearsome snakes, you who cause the bellowing of the bulls, you whose belly is covered with reptilian scales and who carry over your shoulder a woven bag of venomous snakes". She has the eyes of a bull, the voice of a pack of dogs, the calves of a lion, the ankles of a wolf, and she loves fierce dogs: "This is why you are called Hecate of many names, Mene you who split the air like Artemis, shooter of arrows". She is the mother (geneteria) of Gods and men, Nature the universal mother (Phusis panmetor): "You come and go on Olympus and visit the vast and immense Abys: you are the beginning and end, you alone rule over all things; it is in you that all originates, and in you, eternal, that all ends". Another hymn in the Paris codex used as a love charm shows the same joy in piling up titles of the Goddess, who has this time become Venus, the universal procreator (pangenneteria) and mother of Eros, at once below and above, "in the Hells, the Abyss, and the Aeon", chthonic, holding her feats in tombs, and associated with Ereskigal, the Babylonian queen of Hells, but also the "celestial traveler among the stars".

Her ring, scepter and crown represent the power of the one who, possessing the triad, embraces all. Above and below, to the right and to the left, at night as during the day, she is the one "Around whom the nature of the world turns", the very Soul of the world, according to the Chaldaean Oracle "the center in the middle of the Fathers", occupying, according to Psellos, an intermediary position and playing the role of the center in relation to all the other powers: to her left the source of virtues, to her right the source of souls, inside, because she remains within her own substance, but also directed to the outside with a view to procreation.

To the Christian Gnostics, who believed that magic had been brought to earth by angels and spirits, Hecate represents one of the five Archons appointed to rule over the 360 deities of the "Middle," the aerial place below the zodiacal sphere or the circle of the Sun, which fixes the Heimarmene. She has three faces and 27 deities under her command. She occupies the third level in the hierarchy of the "Middle," between two female deities, long-haired Paraplex and Ariouth the Ethiopian, and two male Gods, Typhon and Iachtanabas (Pisitis Sophia).- Roman Book of Laws

This last paragraph reveals that Hecate was seen as the Goddess of Lunar Astrology. In ancient India and Greece, there were 360 days in the year and ancient culture believed a different deity ruled over each day of the year (this is still followed in India to this day). One of the many reasons for Hecate having three faces was based upon her connection to the three major phases of the Moon and the three phases inside the 27 lunar mansions (Palaces). The Moon transits from a South Node mansion to a Mercury mansion three times to complete her journey through the Lunar Zodiac. The 27 deities under her command are the 27 mansions which are addressed in the book "Astrologia Lunaris". Hecate was the Queen of the Night and the Moon, therefore Hecate, the great mystery "Trivia", cannot be anything other than the Goddess of the hidden system of Lunar Astrology.

Hecate in a Birth Chart

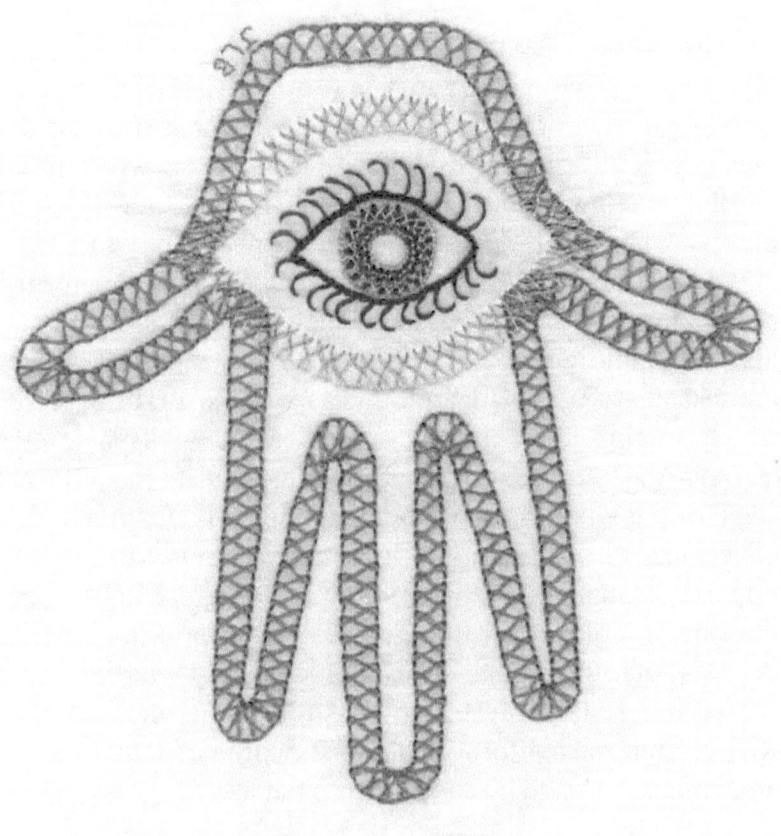

Mark of Hecate (Void of Course)

(All Astrology information is to be seen through sidereal Astrology. All ancient cultures used sidereal NOT Tropical Astrology)

Hecate is the deity that shows up at the moment of pain, suffering, grief, loss, trauma and all difficult transitions. Out of all the forms of the Goddess, Hecate may be the most difficult one to embrace because her work is so utterly human. She is the dark side of the Moon that is involved in all the difficulties a person will have to face, emotional, physical and mental. Hecate has many forms, but her power is in grief, fear, magic, depression, wrath, lust and annihilation. When the Moon or Rising Sign hits the last degree of each Sign and enters the first degree of the following Sign it enters the realm of Hecate (29 degrees to 1 degree of the following Sign), the infernal stage of the Goddess. This can indicate early death, periods of trauma, or intense spiritual awakenings. It is very important to calculate this through the Sidereal Zodiac and not the Tropical, as the Tropical is approximately 23 degrees off the actual constellations. My studies have shown this "Mark of Hecate" is strongest as the Moon or Rising Sign moves through the last degree of Parca Palace and enters the fist degree of Hecate Palace.

Mark of Lucifera (another form of Hecate)

The "Mark of Lucifera" is simple, being born on the New Moon. If the Moon is within 13'20 of the Sun, forward or backward, the Palace and the Qualities of the Palace are destroyed. Example, if the "Mark of Lucifera" is in Vesta Palace, the native born under this mark will lack fire as opposed to possess the fiery traits of Vesta Palace. If this Mark is in the 8th House, 6th House or 12th House it can prove to be fatal or the life of the individual can be plagued with loss or trauma.

Hecate's Palace (home) in the Zodiac

19. HECATE PALACE

Sign: 0' Sagittarius to 13'20 Sagittarius (sidereal)

Lord: South Node

God: Hecate

Sun: December 15th to December 28th

Nature: Infernal

Animal: Dog

Body Part: Left Torso

The symbol of Hecate Palace is a bunch of roots tied together. This Palace signifies everything of basic nature, where motion is finite and limited. Hecate Palace indicates the ideas of foundation, from the very bottom. Hecate Palace people are direct, and prefer to start everything from its core. They are lovers of truth, and are ardent researchers. The Palace deity is Hecate, the Goddess of magic and destruction, thus this Palace can accordingly create many reversals in life. But more often than not, Hecate Palace people with their hard work, shrewdness and ambition, either manage to sidetrack the calamity, or overcome it, emerging as very successful. Hecate Palace is inside the constellation Sagittarius. This is curious to some because Hecate was strongly equated with the constellation Scorpio. The reason for this is due to the "stinger" of the Scorpion falling directly inside this Palace in astronomy.

Hecate Palace's symbol is the "Root" or "Center". This Palace also includes the spiritual center. The symbol is a stylization of Hecate Palace's traditional emblem: a bundle of roots. This bundle of roots represents not only Hecate Palace's urge to seek the essential nature of all things, but also the practice of making medicinal herbs.

Moon/Sun in:

Hecate Palace indicates a person who has a passionate desire to get to the truth and is good at investigation and research. They are direct, ardent and truthful and are shrewd and ambitious, but they can feel trapped and bound by circumstances and may, consequently, feel resentment and a sense of betrayal. They can also suffer extreme reversals of fortune due to Hecate's influence.

Hecate in Literature

Light and dark do not matter when it comes to self realization, one is used to make the other aware. Like the Chinese Yin Yang symbol, inside the heart of light is darkness and inside the heart of darkness is light. Hecate is the darkness that brings the heart the ultimate experience of light. - Jade Sol Luna

HECATE was the goddess of magic, the night, the new moon, ghosts, necromancy and crossroads. She had few public temples in the ancient world, however, small household shrines, which were erected to ward off evil and the malevolent powers of witchcraft, were quite common. Her most important cults were those of Eleusis and the island of Samothrake, where she was worshipped as an associate-goddess of the Mysteries.

In classical sculpture Hecate was depicted in one of two ways: either as a woman holding twin torches; or as three woman standing back to back and facing in three directions. According to Pausanias, Alkamenes was the first sculptor to portray her in this so-called Triformis style. There is a good example of an Hecate Trimorphis in the Vatican Museum and also one in Antiquities Museum of Leiden.

Hecate, is the goddess of purifications and expiations, and is accompanied by Stygian dogs. By Phorcos she became the mother of Scylla. There is another very important feature which arose out of the notion of her being an infernal divinity, namely, she was regarded as a spectral being, who at night sent from the lower world all kinds of demons and terrible phantoms, who taught sorcery and witchcraft, who dwelt at places where two roads crossed each other, on tombs, and near the blood of murdered persons. She herself too wanders about with the souls of the dead, and her approach is announced by the whining and howling of dogs. A number of epithets given her by the poets contain allusions to these features of the popular belief, or to her form. She is described as of terrible appearance, either with three bodies or three heads, the one of a horse, the second of a dog, and the third of a lion. (Orph. Argon. 975, &c.; Eustath. ad Hom. pp. 1467, 1714.)

In works of art she was some-times represented as a single being, but sometimes also as a three-headed monster. We find express mention of her worship at Argos and at Athens, where she had a sanctuary under the name of Epipurgidia, on the acropolis, not far from the temple of Nike, small statues or symbolical representations of Hecate (hekataia) were very numerous, especially at Athens, where they stood before or in houses, and on spots where two roads crossed each other; and it would seem that people consulted such Hecataea as oracles. At the close of every month dishes with food were set out for her and other averters of evil at the points where two roads crossed each other; and this food was consumed by poor people. (Aristoph. Plot. 596 ; Plut. Synmpos. vii. 6.) The sacrifices offered to her consisted of dogs, honey, and black female lambs. (Plut Quaest. Rom. 49; Schol. ad Theocrit. ii. 12 ; Apollon. Rhod. iii. 1032.)

HECATE & HERMES

Hecate was probably described as the consort of Khthonian (Underworld) Hermes in the cults of Thessalian Pherai and Eleusis. Both gods were leaders of the ghosts of the dead, and were associated with the spring-time return of Persephone. Then still remembering her ancient ills, she howled in sorrow through the land of Thrace. That fate of hers stirred pity in the hearts of friend and foe, Trojans and Greeks alike, and all the gods as well--all: Juno Ovid, Metamorphoses 7.362 ff :

"Past the tomb of Paris [in the Troad] buried in the shallow sand; the meadowlands that Maera terrified with monstrous barks [N.B. Ovid connects Hekabe or Hecate with the dog-star Seirios or Maira]."

HECATE GODDESS OF THE NIGHT

Hecate was a torch-bearing goddess of the night, the leader of haunting ghosts and inspirer of the night-time baying of hounds. She may have been a goddess of the moon or rather of moonless starlit nights.

"Hecate ... pleased with dark ghosts that wander through the shade ... nightly seen." - Orphic Hymn 1 to Hecate

"Propitiating the only-begotten Maiden (Koure mounogeneia) [Hecate] with a midnight offering ... Brimo [Hecate], nurse of youth (kourotrophos), Brimo, night-wanderer of the underworld (nyktipolis khthonie), Queen of the dead (anassa eneroi)." - Apollonius Rhodius, Argonautica 3.840

"Hecate Brimo ... hearing his words from the abyss, came up ... She was garlanded by fearsome snakes that coiled themselves round twigs of oak; the twinkle of a thousand torches lit the scene; and hounds of the underworld barked shrilly all around her." - Apollonius Rhodius, Argonautica 3.1194

"[Selene the Moon cries:] 'How many times ... have you [the witch Medea] adored me with your incantations, making the night moonless so that you might practise your beloved witchcraft undisturbed." - Apollonius Rhodius, Argonautica 4.55
[NB Hecate empowered witches with the power to draw down the moon.]

"In the deep stillness of the midnight hour ... she [Medea] stretched her arms to the stars ... O Nox [Nyx the Night], Mother of Mysteries, and all ye golden Astra (Stars) who with Luna [Selene the Moon] succeed the fires of day, and thou, divine triceps (three-formed) Hecate, who knowest all my enterprises and dost fortify the arts of magic." - Ovid, Metamorphoses 7.162

"Out of Erebos and Chaos she called Nox (Night) and the Di Nocti (Gods of Night) and poured a prayer with long-drawn wailing cries to Hecate." - Ovid, Metamorphoses 10.403

"Hecate, Queen of the Night." - Valerius Flaccus, Argonautica 7.515

"Dionysos waited for darksome night, and appealed in these words to circle Mene (Moon) in heaven: 'O daughter of Helios (Sun), Mene (Moon) of many turnings, nurse of all! O Selene (Moon), driver of the silver car! If thou art Hecate of many names, if in the night thou doest shake thy mystic torch in brandcarrying hand, come nightwanderer, nurse of puppies because the nightly sound of the hurrying dogs is thy delight with their mournful whimpering." - Nonnus, Dionysiaca 44.198

GODDESS OF NECROMANCY & GHOSTS

The gods Hecate, Persephone and Haides presided over the oracles of the dead and the art of nekromankia (necromancy), the summoning forth of the ghosts of the dead.

Hecate led the ghosts of the dead to the upper world at night. Her passing was heralded by the baying of dogs.

"The lady Hecate was minister and companion to Persephone [goddess of the underworld]." - Homeric Hymn 2 to Demeter 436

Aeschylus, Doubtul Fragment 249 (from Plutarch, On Superstition 3. 166A) (trans. Weir Smyth) (Greek tragedy C5th B.C.) :
"But either thou art frightened of a spectre (phantasma) beheld in sleep and hast joined the revel-rout of nether (chthonia) Hecate."

"Hecate, night-wanderer of the underworld (nyktipolis khthonie), Queen of the dead (anassa eneroi)." - Apollonius Rhodius, Argonautica 3.840

"Hecate ... pleased with dark ghosts that wander through the shade; Perseis, solitary goddess." - Orphic Hymn 1 to Hecate

"Out of Erebos and Chaos she called Nox (Night) and the Di Nocti (Gods of Night) and poured a prayer with long-drawn wailing cries to Hecate ... a groan came from the ground, the bushes blanched, the spattered sward was soaked with gouts of blood, stones brayed and bellowed, dogs began to bark, black snakes swarmed on the soil and ghostly shapes of silent spirits floated through the air." - Ovid, Metamorphoses 10.403

"Baying [of Hounds] loud as that which rings at the grim gate of Dis [Haides] or from Hecate's escort [of black hounds] to the world above." - Valerius Flaccus, Argonautica 6.110 "At another time you [Egyptian Isis] are Hecate, whose howls at night inspire dread, and whose triple form restrains the emergence of ghosts as you keep the entrance to the earth above firmly barred. You wander through diverse groves, and are appeased by various rites." - Apuleius, Golden Ass 11.218

NECROMANCY OF THE CUMAEAN SIBYLLA & AENEAS

The Cumaean Sibyl guided Aeneas to the Underworld through the Oracle of the Dead near Cumae. Virgil's account of the story is partially quoted here.

"The Sibyl [performing the rites of necromankia at the oracle of the dead at Cumae] first lined up four black-skinned bullocks, poured a libation wine upon their foreheads, and then, plucking the topmost hairs from between their brows, she placed these on the altar fires as an initial offering, calling aloud upon Hecate, powerful in heaven and hell. While other laid their knives to these victim's throats, and caught the fresh warm blood in bowls, Aeneas sacrifices a black-fleeced lamb to Nox (Night), the mother of the Furiae, and her great sister, Terra (earth), and a barren heifer to Proserpine.

Then he [Aeneas] set up altars by night to the god of the Underworld [Hades], laying upon the flames whole carcases of bulls and pouring out rich oil over the burning entrails. But listen! - at the very first crack of dawn, the ground underfoot began to mutter, the woody ridges to quake, and a baying of hounds was heard through the half-light: the goddess was coming, Hecate. [a path then opened up for the Sibyl & Aeneas to travel down to Hades]." - Virgil, Aeneid 6.257

NECROMANCY OF AESON & ALKIMEDE

Aeson and his wife, the witch Alkimede, are here described performing necromancy to learn from the ghosts of the dead the fate of their son Jason, and also to bring down the curses of the dead upon King Pelias, who has sentenced them to death.

"Unto the lord of Tartarus [Hades] and unto the Stygian ghosts was Alcimede [mother of Jason] bringing holy offerings in fear for her mighty son [the Argonaut Jason], if Shades summoned forth [using the magic of Nekromankia] might give her surer knowledge. Even Aeson himself, who shares her anxiety but who hides such unmanly fears in his heart, yields and is led by his wife. In a trench stands blood and plenteous offering to hidden

Phlegethon and with fierce cries the aged witch calls upon her departed ancestors and the grandson of great Pleione [Hermes guide of souls]. And now at the sound of the spell rose a face, insubstantial, and [the ghost of] Kretheus gazed upon his mournful son and daughter-in-law, and when he had sipped the blood he began to utter these words [tells him that Jason is safe, but King Pelias is plotting Aeson's death] ... He [Aeson] returns to the holy rites [of the Underworld Gods]. Beneath the gloom of an ancient cypress, squalid and ghastly wi th darksome hue, a bull still stood, dark blue fillets on his horns, his brow rough with the foliage of yew; the beast too was downcast, panting and restless, and terrified at the sight of the shade. The witch [Alkimede], according to the custom of her evil race had kept him, chosen above all others, to use him now at last for these hellish practises.

When Aeson saw that the bull still remained at the hour of the awful rites unslain, he dooms him to death, and with one hand upon the horns of the fated victim speaks for the last time [cursing his half-brother King Pelias] ... Then he appeased the goddess of triple form [Hecate goddess of earthly ghosts], and with his last sacrifice offers a prayer to the Stygian abodes, rehearsing backward a spell soon, soon to prove persuasive; for without that no thin shade will the dark ferryman [Kharon] take away, and bound they stand at the mouth of Orcus [Haides]." - Valerius Flaccus, Argonautica 1.730

NECROMANCY OF TEIRESIAS

In the following passage the seer Teiresias performing necromancy to commune with the ghosts of the dead. The ghost of the same seer is consulted by Odysseus in Homer's Odyssey.

"[The seer Teiresias performs necromancy:] Loud bayed the pack of Hecate; thrice the deep valley gave out a mournful noise; the whole place was shaken and the ground was stricken from below. `My prayers are heard,' says the priest; `prevailing words I uttered; blind Chaos is burst open, and for the tribes of Dis [Haides] a way is given to the upper world.'" - Seneca, Oedipus 569

"There stands a wood, enduring of time, and strong and erect in age, with foliage aye unshorn nor pierced by any suns ... Nor do the shadows lack a divine power: Latonia's [Artemis-Hecates'] haunting presence is added to the grove ... Her arrows whistle unseen through the wood, her hounds bay nightly, when she flies from her uncle's [Haides'] threshold and resumes afresh Diana's kindlier shape [Diana is here regarded as a dual Artemis-Hecate] ... [Teiresias performing the rites of nekromankia] bids the dark-fleeced sheep and black oxen be set before him ...

Then he entwined their fierce horns with wreaths of dusky hue, handling them himself, and first at the edge of that well-known wood [sacred to Hecate] he nine times spills the lavish draughts of Bacchus into a hollowed trench, and gifts of vernal milk and Attic rain [honey] and propitiatory blood to the Shades below; so much is poured out as the dry earth will drink. Then they roll tree trunks thither, and the sad priest bids there be three altar-fires for Hecate and three for the maidens born of cursed Acheron [the Erinyes]; for thee, lord of Avernus [Haides], a heap of pinewood though sunk into the ground yet towers high into the air; next to this an altar of lesser bulk is raised to Ceres of the Underworld [Persephone]; in front and on every side the cypress of lamentation intertwines them. And now, their lofty heads marked with the sword and the pure sprinkled meal, the cattle fell under the stroke; then the virgin Manto [daughter of Teiresias], catching the blood in bowls, makes first libation, and moving thrice round all the pyres, as her holy sire commands, offers the half-dead tissues and yet living entrails, nor delays to set the devouring fire to the dark foliage. And when Tiresias heard the branches crackling in the flames and the grim piles roaring - for the burning heat surges before his face, and the fiery vapour fills the hollows of his eyes - he exclaimed, and the pyres trembled, and the flames cowered at his voice: 'Abodes of Tartarus and awful realm of insatiable Mors [Thanatos, death], and thou, most cruel of the brothers [Haides], to whom the Shades are given to serve thee, and the eternal punishments of the damned obey thee, and the palace of the underworld, throw open in answer to my knowing the silent places and empty void of stern Persephone, and send forth the multitude that lurk in hollow night; let the ferryman [Kharon] row back across the Styx with groaning bark.

Haste ye all together, nor let there be fore the Shades but one fashion of return to the light; do thou, daughter of

Perses [Hecate], and the cloud-wrapt Arcaidan [Hermes] with rod of power lead in separate throng the pious denizens of Elysium; but for those who died in crime, who in Erebus, as among the seed of Cadmus, are most in number, be thou their leader, Tisiphone, go on before with snake thrice brandished and blazing yew-branch, and throw open the light of day, nor let Cerberus interpose his heads, and turn aside the ghosts that lack the light." - Statius, Thebaid 4.410

HECATE GODDESS OF WITCHCRAFT

"We are told that Helios (the Sun) had two sons, Aeetes and Perses, Aeetes being the king of Kolkhis and the other king of the Tauric Chersonese, and that both of them were exceedingly cruel. And Perses had a daughter Hecate, who surpassed her father in boldness and lawlessness; she was also fond of hunting, and when she had no luck she would turn her arrows upon human beings instead of the beasts. Being likewise ingenious in the mixing of deadly poisons she discovered the drug called aconite and tired out the strength of each poison by mixing it with food given to the strangers. And since she possessed great experience in such matters she first of all poisoned her father, and so succeeded to the throne, and then, founding a temple of Artemis and commanding that strangers who landed there should be sacrificed to the goddess, she became know far and wide for her cruelty. After this she married Aeetes and bore two daughters, Kirke and Medea, and a son Aigialeus. Although Kirke also, it is said devoted herself to the devising of all kinds of drugs and discovered roots of all=2

0manner of natures and potencies such as are difficult to credit, yet, notwithstanding that she was taught by her mother Hecate about not a few drugs ... Aeetes, partly because of his own natural cruelty and partly because he was under the influence of his wife Hecate, had given his approval to the custom of slaying strangers. But since Medea as time went on opposed the purpose of her parents more and more, Aeetes, they say, suspecting his daughter of plotting against him consigned her to free custody [that is, on parole]; Medea, however, made her escape and fled for refuge to a sacred precinct of Helios on the shore of the sea." - Diodorus Siculus, Library of History 4.45.1

MAGIC OF THE WITCH MEDEA

Hecate was the source of the magical power of the witch Medea. Most of her magic is described as nocturnal and / or necromantic.

"[Medea curses Jason who plans to abandon her and marry Glauke:] 'By the goddess I worship most of all, my chosen helper Hecate, who dwells in the inner chamber of my house [household shrine], none of them shall pain my heart and smile at it! Bitter will I make their marriage, bitter Kreon's marriage-alliance, and bitter my banishment from the land!" - Euripides, Medea 396

"As a rule she [Medea] did=2 0not spend her time at home, but was busy all day in the temple of Hecate, of whom she was priestess." - Apollonius Rhodius, Argonautica 3.250

"[Argos, nephew of Medea, to Jason:] 'You have heard me speak of a young woman [Medea] who practices witchcraft under the tutelage of the goddess Hecate. If we could win her over, we might banish from our minds all fear of your defeat in the ordeal [yoking the fire breathing bulls of Aeetes]." - Apollonius Rhodius, Argonautica 3.478

"[Argos, nephew of Medea, to the Argonauts:] 'There is a girl [Medea] living in Aeetes' palace whom the goddess Hecate has taught to handle with extraordinary skill all the magic herbs that grow on dry land or in running water. With these she can put out a raging fire, she can stop rivers as they roar in spate, arrest a star, and check the movement of the sacred moon." - Apollonius Rhodius, Argonautica 3.529

"[Medea prays to Hecate]: And yet I wish he [Jason] had been spared. Yes Sovran Lady Hecate, this is my prayer. Let him live to reach his home." - Apollonius Rhodius, Argonautica 3.466

"[Medea persuaded by her aunt Khalkiope to help Jason:] 'At dawn I will go to Hecate's temple with magic medicine for the bulls [to protect Iason from their fiery breath]." - Apollonius Rhodius, Argonautica 3.735

"She [Medea] wished to drive to the splendid Temple of Hecate [in Kolkhis]; and while they [her handmaidens] were getting the=2 0carriage ready she took a magic ointment from her box. This salve was named after Prometheus. A man had only to smear it on his body, after propitiating the only-begotten Maiden (Koure mounogenes) [Hecate] with a midnight offering, to become invulnerable by sword or fire and for that day to surpass himself in strength and daring. It first appeared in a plant that sprang from the blood-like ichor of Prometheus in his torment, which the flesh-eating eagle had dropped on the spurs of Kaukasos ... To make the ointment, Medea, clothed in black, in the gloom of night, had drawn off this juice in a Caspian shell after bathing in seven perennial streams and calling seven times on Brimo [Hecate], nurse of youth (kourotrophos), Brimo, night-wanderer of the underworld (nyktipolis khthonie), Queen of the dead (anassa eneroi). The dark earth shook and rumbled underneath the Titan root when it was cut, and Prometheus himself groaned in the anguish of his soul." - Apollonius Rhodius, Argonautica 3.840

"[Medea to Iason:] Medea forced herself to speak to him. 'Hear me now,' she said. 'These are my plans for you. When you have met my father and has given you the deadly teeth from the serpent's jaws, wait for the moment of midnight and after bathing in an ever-running river, go out alone in sombre clothes and dig a round pit in the earth. There, kill a ewe and after heaping up a pure over the pit, sacrifice it whole, with a libation of honey from the hive and prayers to Hecate, Perses' only daughter (mounogenes). Then, when you have invoked the goddess duly, withdraw from the pyre.

And to not be tempted to look behind you as you go, either by footfalls or the baying of hounds, or you may ruin everything and never reach your friends alive. In the morning, melt this charm, strip, and using it like oil, anoint your body. It will endow you with tremendous strength and boundless confidence ... neither the spear-points of the earthborn men nor the consuming flames that the savage bulls spew out will find you vulnerable." - Apollonius Rhodius, Argonautica 3.1022

"Iason waited for the bright constellation of the Bear to decline, and then, when all the air from heaven to earth was still, he set out like a stealthy thief across the solitary plain. During the day he had prepared himself, and so had everything he needed with him; Argos had fetched him some milk and a ewe from a farm; the rest he had taken from the ship itself. When he had found an unfrequented spot in a clear meadow under the open sky, he began by bathing his naked body reverently in the sacred river, and then put on a dark mantle which Hypsipyle of Lemnos had given him to remind him of their passionate embraces. Then he dug a pit a cubit deep, piled up billets, and laid the sheep on top of them after cutting its throat. He kindled the wood from underneath and poured mingled libations on the sacrifice, calling on Hecate to help him in the coming test. This done, he withdrew; and the dread goddess (thea deinos), hearing his words from the abyss, came up to accept the offering of Iason's son. She was garlanded by fearsome snakes that coiled themselves round twigs of oak; the twinkle of a thousand torches lit the scene; and hounds of the underworld barked shrilly all around her. The whole meadow trembled under her feet, and the Nymphai of marsh and river who haunt the fens by Amarantian Phasis cried out in fear. Iason was terrified;

but even so, as he retreated, he did not once turn round. And so he found himself among his friends once more, and Dawn arrived." - Apollonius Rhodius, Argonautica 3.1194

"The beautiful Medea sped through the palace, and for her the very doors responding to her hasty incantations swung open of their own accord." - Apollonius Rhodius, Argonautica 4.39

Then she returned; the Dracones, though untouched save by the wafting odour of those herbs, yet sloughed their aged skins of many years. Before the doors she stopped nor crossed the threshold; only the heavens covered her; she shunned Jason's embrace; then two turf altars built, the right to Hecate, the left to Juventas [Hebe goddess of Youth], wreathed with the forest's mystic foliage, and dug two trenches in the ground beside and then performed her rites. Plunging a knife into a black sheep's throat she drenched the wide ditches with blood; next from a c halice poured a stream of wine and from a second chalice warm frothing milk and, chanting magic words, summoned the Numina Terrena (Deities of Earth) and prayed the sad shades' monarch (Rex Umbrarum) [Haides] and his stolen bride [Persephone] that, of their mercy, from old Aeson's frame they will not haste to steal the breath of life. And when in long low-murmured supplications the deities were appeased, she bade bring out the old exhausted king [Aeson], and with a spell charmed him to deepest sleep and laid his body, lifeless it seemed, stretched on a bed of herbs. Away! She ordered Jason and away! The ministrants, and warned that eyes profane see not her secrets; then with streaming hair, ecstatic round the flaming altars moved, and in the troughs of flood dipped cloven stakes and lit them dripping at the flames, and thrice with water, thrice with sulphur, thrice with fire purged the pale sleeping body of the king. Meanwhile within the deep bronze cauldron, white with bubbling froth, the rich elixir boils. Roots from the vales of Thessaly and seeds and flowers she seethes therein and bitter juices, with gem-stones from the farthest Orient and sands that Oceanus' ebbing waters wash, and hoar-frost gathered when the moon shines full, and wings and flesh of owls and the warm guts of wolves that change at will to human form. To them she adds the slender scaly skins of Libyan water-snakes and then the livers of long-lived gazelles and eggs and heads of ancient crows, nine generations old.20 With these and a thousand other nameless things her more than mortal purpose she prepared. Then with a seasoned stick of olive wood she mixed the whole and stirred it.

And behold! The old dry stick that stirred the bubbling brew grew green and suddenly burst into leaf, and all at once was laden with fat olives; and where the froth flowed over from the pot and the hot drops spattered the ground beneath, fair springtime bloomed again, and everywhere flowers of the meadow sprang and pasture sweet. And seeing this Medea drew her blade and slit the old king's throat and let the blood run out and filled his veins and arteries with her elixir; and when Aeson drank, through wound and lips, at once his hair and beard, white for long years, regained their raven hue; his wizened pallor, vanquished, fled away and firm new flesh his sunken wrinkles filled, and all his limbs were sleek and proud and strong. Then Aeson woke and marvelled as he saw his prime restored of forty years before." - Ovid, Metamorphoses 7.162

MAGIC OF THE WITCH KIRKE

"She [Hecate] married Aeetes and bore two daughters, Kirke and Medea, and a son Aigialeus. Although Kirke also, it is said devoted herself to the devising of all kinds of drugs and discovered roots of all manner of natures and potencies such as are difficult to credit, yet, notwithstanding that she was taught by her mother Hecate about not a few drugs." - Diodorus Siculus, Library of History 4.45.1

"Then Circe turned to prayers and incantations, and unknown chants to worship unknown gods, chants which she used to eclipse Luna's (the Moon's) pale face and veil her father's [the Sun's] orb in thirsty clouds. Now too the heavens are darkened as she sings; the earth breathes vapours ... They [Picus' courtiers] changed on Circe (who by now=2 0had cleared the air and let the wind and sun disperse the mists) and charged her, rightly, with her guilt and claimed their king and threatened force and aimed their angry spears. She sprinkled round about her evil drugs and poisonous essences, and out of Erebos and Chaos called Nox (Night) and the Di Nocti (Gods of Night) and poured a prayer with long-drawn wailing cries to Hecate. The woods (wonder of wonders!) leapt away, a groan came from the ground, the bushes blanched, the spattered sward was soaked with gouts of blood, stones brayed and bellowed, dogs began to bark, black snakes swarmed on the soil and ghostly shapes of silent spirits floated through the air. The woods (wonder of wonders!) leaps away, a groan came from the ground, the bushes blanched, the spattered sward was soaked with gouts of blood, stones brayed and bellowed, dogs began to bar, black snakes searmed on the solid and ghostly shapes of silent spirits floated through the air. Stunned by such magic sorcery, the group of courtiers stood aghast; and as they gazes, she touched their faces with her poisoned wand, and at its touch each took the magic form of some wild beast; none kept his proper shape." - Ovid, Metamorphoses 14.369

HECATE IDENTIFIED WITH ARTEMIS

Artemis was frequently identified with the goddess Hecate. In the Homeric Hymn to Demeter, Artemis the playmate of Persephone perhaps becomes Hecate, the companion of Demeter in the search for her stolen daughter. Hekatos (the far-shooter) was also a common Homeric epithet applied to Artemis' brother Apollon. Depictions of the two goddesses were near identical. The attributes they had in common included a short-skirt and hunting boots, torches and a hunting dog.

"We pray that other guardians be always renewed, and that Artemis-Hecate watch over the childbirth of their women." - Aeschylus, Suppliant Women 674

"O Artemis, thou maid divine, Diktynna, huntress, fair to see, O bring that keen-nosed pack of thine, and hunt through all the house with me. O Hecate, with flameful brands." - Aristophanes, Frogs 1358

"Aeetes succeeded to the throne, and then, founding a temple of Artemis [usually described as a temple of Hecate, but the author equates the two] and commanding that strangers who landed there should be sacrificed to the goddess." - Diodorus Siculus, Library of History 4.45.1

TRIAD OF HECATE, ARTEMIS & SELENE

The triad Hecate-Artemis-Selene was popular in Roman-era poetry.

"[Medea cries out to Hecate:] `Thou [Hecate-Selene] who doest show thy bright face as witness of the silent mysteries, O three-formed (triformis) Hecate.'" - Seneca, Medea 6

"[The witch Medea casts her spells:] `Now, summoned by my sacred rites, do thou [Hecate], orb of the night [i.e. the moon], put on thy most evil face and come, threatening in all thy forms." - Seneca, Medea 750

"The hour is at hand, O Phoebe [Hecate-Selene], for thy sacred rites." - Seneca, Medea 770

"[The witch Medea summons the power of Hecate:] `I see Trivia's [Hecate-Selene-Artemis] swift gliding car, not as when, radiant, with full face [i.e. the moon], she drives the livelong night, but as when, ghastly, with mournful aspect, harried by Thessalian threats, she skirts with nearer rein the edge of heaven. So do thou wanly shed form thy torch a gloomy light through air; terrify the peoples with new dread, and let precious Corinthian bronzes resound, Dictynna [Artemis-Selene], to thy aid. To thee on the altar's bloody turf we perform thy solemn rites." - Seneca, Medea 787

"[Phaedra prays to Artemis-Hecate-Selene:] `O [Artemis] queen of the groves (regina nemorum), thou who in solitude lovest thy mountain-haunts, and who upon the solitary mountains art alone held holy, change for the better these dark, ill-omened threats. O great goddess of the woods and groves, bright orb of heaven, glory of the night, by whose changing beams the universe shines clear, O three-formed Hecate, lo, thou art at hand,=2 0favouring our undertaking. Conquer the unbending soul of stern Hippolytus; may he, compliant, give ear unto our prayer. Soften his fierce heart; may he learn to love, may he feel answering flames. Ensnare his mind; grim, hostile, fierce, may he turn him back unto the fealty of love.

To this end direct thy powers; so mayst thou wear a shining face [Selene the moon] and, the clouds all scattered, fare on with undimmed horns; so, when thou drivest thy car through the nightly skies, may no witcheries of Thessaly prevail to drag thee down and may no shepherd [i.e. Endymion] make boast o'er thee. Be near, goddess, in answer to our call; hear now our prayers." - Seneca, Phaedra 406

"With such swift course as the lord [Helios the sun] of stars hurries on the centuries, and in such wise as Hecate [Selene the moon] hastens along her slanting ways." - Seneca, Troades 386

"[Statius, in the passage that follows describes Artemis as a triple goddess incorporating: Artemis-Hecate-Selene:] Cynthia, queen of the mysteries of the night, if as they say thou dost vary in threefold wise the aspect of thy godhead, and in different shape comest down into the woodland ... The goddess stooped her horns and made bright her kindly star, and illumined the battle-field with near-approaching chariot." - Statius, Thebaid 10.365

Hecate in Chaldaean Oracles

Her three forms (*trimorphos* PGM XXXVI, 190) and her three faces (*triposopos*, IV, 2119, 2880) make her, as in classical Greek tradition, the goddess of crossroads (*triodites*) and the protectress of roads; but they express above all the "abundance of all magical signs" (XXXVI, 190-191), possessed by the "sovereign" goddess (*kuria*, IV, 1432) "of many names" (*poluonumos*, IV, 745). The three-faced Hecate of the love charm of Pitys, contained in the magical Greek codex of Paris, has the head of a cow on the right, the head of a female dog on the left, and the head of a girl in the center (IV, 2120-2123). The Hecate engraved in a magnetized rock (IV, 2881-2884) also shows three faces: a goat on the right, a female dog on the left, and in the middle a girl with horns.

Her mouth exhales fire (*puripnoa*, IV, 2727); her six hands brandish torches (IV, 2119-2120). Hence, engraving her name with a bronze stylus on an ostracon (XXXVI, 189) or on a lead tablet (IV, 2956) will have the effect of a fire "burning" and "consuming" the beloved woman, so that she is deprived of sleep forever. Furthermore, the fire that inhabits Hecate, as the most subtle of the four elements, characterizes her keen intelligence and the extreme sharpness of her perception (*puriboulos*, IV, 2751). Her whole being radiates with the brilliance of the fire from the stars and from the ether. The *Chaldaean Oracles* made this Hecate "of the breasts that welcome storms, of resplendent brilliance" into an entity "descended from the Father," associated with the "implacable thunderbolts" of the gods, with the "flower of fire," and with the "powerful breath" of the paternal Intellect.

Because she caries and transmits fire from above, she is the supreme goddess of vivification. The reason Hecate's womb is so remarkably "fertile" (*zoogonon*) is that she is filled with the fire of paternal Intellect, the source of life or the strength of thought, which it is her duty to communicate and to disseminate. Through her emblems and her triadic conception, Hecate is associated with another goddess o time and destiny, Mene or Selene, the goddess of the moon. A prayer to the moon invokes them as one and the same entity; epithets and attributes of the two goddesses are interchangeable. Hecate/Selene also has three heads, carries torches, presides over crossroads: "You who in the three forms of the three Charites dance and fly about with the stars . . . You who wield terrible black torches in your hands, you who shake your head with hair made of fearsome snakes, you who cause the bellowing of the bulls, you whose belly is covered with reptilian scales and who carry over your shoulder a woven bag of venomous snakes" (IV, 2793-2806). She has the eye of a bull, the voice of a pack of dogs, the calves of a lion, the ankles of a wolf, and she loves fierce bitches: "This is why you are called Hecate of many names, Mene you who split the air like Artemis, shooter of arrows" (IV, 2814-2817). She is the mother (*geneteria*) of gods and men, Nature the universal mother (*Phusis panmetor*): "You come and go on Olympus and visit the vast and immense Abys: you are the beginning and end, you alone rule over all things; it is in you that all originates, and in you, eternal, that all ends" (IV, 2832-2839). Another hymn in the Paris codex used as a love charm shows the same joy in piling up titles of the goddess, who has this time become Aphrodite, the universal procreator (*pangenneteria*) and mother of Eros (IV, 2556-2557), at once below and above, "in the Hells, the Abys, and the Aeon" (IV, 256-2564), chthonic, holding her feats in tombs, and associated with Ereskigal, the Babylonian queen of Hells (LXX, 4), but also the "celestial traveler among the stars" (IV, 2549-2550).Her ring, scepter and crown represent the power of the one who, possessing the triad, embraces all. Above and below, to the right and to the left, at night as during the day, she is the one "Around whom the nature of the world turns" (IV, 2551-2552), the very Soul of the world, according to the Chaldaean Oracle "the center in the middle of the Fathers", occupying, according to Psellos, an intermediary position and playing the role of the center in relation to all the other powers: t her left the source of virtues, to her right the source of souls, inside, because she remains within her own substance, but also directed to the outside with a view to procreation.

Whether invoked in love charms to bring to oneself the woman one desires (the *agogai* of the magic papyruses) or *theiodamoi anankai* of the Chaldaean philosophers, Hecate is henceforth inscribed in a table of correspondences and combinations which go far beyond her proper function as a goddess of enchantment and magic. It is from this Hecate, the product of the syncretism of the papyri, that the tradition of the Hecate of the Neoplatonic commentators on the *Oracles* take shape.

"Illusion of Death" inspired by Swami Shivananda

"Hecate in Literature"

Hesiod, Theogony - Greek Epic C8th-7th B.C.

The Homeric Library - Greek Mythography C2nd A.D.

Apollonius Rhodius, The Argonautica - Greek Epic C3rd B.C.

Lycophron, Alexandra - Greek Poetry C3rd B.C.

Pausanias, Description of Greece - Greek Geography C2nd A.D.

Diodorus Siculus, The Library of History - Greek History C1st B.C.

Antoninus Liberalis, Metamorphoses - Greek Mythography C2nd A.D.

Aelian, On Animals - Greek Natural History C2nd - C3rd A.D.

Ovid, Metamorphoses - Latin Epic C1st BC - C1st A.D. Hymns - Greek Epic C8th-4th B.C.

Greek Lyric IV Bacchylides, Fragments - Greek Lyric C5th B.C.

Apollodorus

The Mystic and Cerberus

(Seminar Virginia 2005)

Hesiod tells of a goddess named Echidna (often equated with Hecate), "the serpent", a daughter of the "Old Ones of the Sea", Phorkys and Keto. She was born in a cave, half beautiful-cheeked, bright-eyed woman, half terrible huge snake, thrashing about in the hollows of the earth and devouring her victims raw. The immortals assigned her a dwelling place beneath a rock far from gods and men, in a place called Arima, also called "the couch of Typhoeus", her husband.

Her husband, the dragon Typhoeus, or Typhon, was the youngest, strongest, and most colossal of all Gaia's children, born after Zeus's conquest of the Titans. Above the hips he was shaped like a man, and was so tall that he overtopped the highest mountain and his head often knocked against the stars. One of his arms extended to the sunset and the other to the sunrise. From his shoulders grew a hundred heads of serpents, sometimes baying like a dog, or making the mountains echo with their hiss. From the hips downwards he was shaped like two wrestling serpents, which towered up to the height of his head and screamed hissingly. His entire body was covered with wings and from his mouth spurted flames instead of spittle.

In the darkness of the caves at Arima, many monsters were born to these two creatures, and among them was the terrible hound Cerberus.

Cerberus is said in later accounts to be a ferocious hound with three heads, three gaping growling jaws with frightful teeth, and drool that, upon touching the earth, sprouts the poisonous wolf-bane herb (aconite). Earlier descriptions by Hesiod reveal that the lower half of his body was that of a serpent, like his mother, that many venomous serpents heads sprout from his back and that he has in fact, fifty growling and baying heads.

Cerberus is famous as the archetypal hell hound, guard dog to the Underworld, guardian of his beloved master Hades and of Persephone, Queen of the Dead. The dead he welcomes with the warmth and innocence of a friendly and trusting pet, but he shows no mercy, and devours immediately any that try to escape the Underworld without his master's consent. Likewise, the living are usually frightened away from the realms of the dead by this foul beast, though there are cases where some have been literally frightened to death at the sight of him, others consumed by lingering and violent madness. (see Tales of Dr. Taverner by Dion Fortune for a dramatic example.) The only creatures known to regularly pass Cerberus without confrontation are Hermes and Hecate, the two known guides of the Underworld.

One of the twelve heroic acts of Hercules was to overpower Cerberus without the use of weapons and carry him out into the open world, having first obtained permission from Hades. In this tale we see how even the archetypal hero had to use all his strength of character and sheer "guts" to bring this horrible creature out into the open and face it full force in naked daylight. It is interesting to note too, that no sooner did Hercules let him go, than did Cerberus quickly slink back into the bowls of the earth again, to stand his post at the Gates of Death.

In one tale, it is said that Demeter entered the Underworld herself, in search of her abducted daughter, and was able to distract Cerberus by throwing him some drugged cakes, and thus pass un-noticed. Tales tell of others who distracted Cerberus by playing sweet music, which calmed and enchanted the ferocious beast, and so entranced him that he did not notice them slipping past.

It has been my own experience, traveling the Path of Hecate, in meeting Cerberus at the feet of his masters throne, that Cerberus indeed was terrifying, but his master took charge of me as a guest and Cerberus seems to have followed his master's cue. Remarkably though, after my gaze into the mirror in the hall of death, Cerberus became a friendly guide/teacher and lead me to the most beautiful and intimate experience of Saturnus Caelum! After this experience, I saw the terrible Cerberus running and barking and playing with his master, almost like a puppy, and certainly in love!

How is it that we mystics are able to pass Cerberus so easily? This is the grace of worshipping Hecate. How is it that Cerberus is transformed for us from a creature capable of driving one to madness and suicide, into a loving companion with a lot to show us and a lot to teach us? Again, this is the grace of Mother Hecate.

The assistance of Hecate is unparallel to any other underworld goddess. This journey through the Caelums has been carefully and lovingly orchestrated for us by our teacher Hecate, who guides us like Hermes through each experience. The astral pathworking also bears the graces of other beings like Typhon, Luna, Diana, Hades, and Persephone, who kindly welcome us and help us through the experience. Perhaps the real-life confrontation with Cerberus is more difficult, because like Hercules, we must ultimately face him alone and without weapons. Perhaps we can find in Hecate, the secret to such strength.

STYX: The Threshold of the Underworld

Far distant from the gods lives the Hated Goddess, Styx, in her famous palace beneath a high rock. There the sky is supported by pillars of silver. Hecate seldom journeys thither, over the wide plains of the sea. But if dissension and strife break out amongst the immortals, and if some dweller on Olympus takes refuge in a lie, then Zeus sends Hecate to fetch the mighty Oath Of The Gods. She fetches it from afar, in a golden goblet, that cold water, known by many names, which gushes down from the high rock. It is the water of Styx. Like all other waters, this water, too, pours beneath the earth, in deep night, from the horn of Okeanos. It's stream is divided into ten parts. Nine arms encompass the earth and sea: the tenth arm flows from this rock, to the hurt of the gods. For whoever of them perjures himself by this water, he is at once struck down and lies unbreathing a whole year long. He comes no more to the ambrosia and nectar, to the food and drink of the immortals, but remains dumb and aswoon in his abode. After the end of the year, other and heavier punishments await him. For nine years he is banished from the councils and revels of the gods. Only in the tenth year may he again take part in their assemblies.

Beginning with the underworld Path, we are embarking on a long and difficult journey, exploring the inner realms to understand our true nature, and that of the world around us. It could be said that this path, being the first one we explore, represents the pathworking itself and shows us what will happen in the entire journey ahead.

Entering your shadow self is the act of entering the Underworld, of searching within ourselves to know ourselves better, and of searching "behind the scenes" to know the world better.

As a general rule, we may interpret living beings throughout the Paths as aspects of ourselves, and inanimate objects as aspects of our world, or our environment.

In the world around us, there are certain limitations to what people will see or discuss, to what is socially acceptable. This boundary, like the river Styx which surrounds the Underworld, is inevitably defined by what people hate to talk about or address (hate is the meaning of the word "Styx"). Some examples of problems too huge to be comfortable with might be, suffering, violent death, lunacy and separation. To this short list we could even add that fact that those who challenge us by acting out of ignorance, are feeling, emotional, living gods on earth, each in their own right, even if they are ignoring huge and painful parts of themselves too. Equally banished across the boundary of acceptability are inexplicable phenomena in our immediate experience. These are phenomena which we, as a culture, deliberately try to convince ourselves and each other that they do not happen, they do not exist. Examples include subjects belonging to Hecate such as, underworld deities, ghosts, spirits, death and suffering. A person who crosses the line of any of these uncomfortable subjects (like one who breaks an oath sworn on the Styx) is said to be rough, or coarse, and is often shunned and left alone like the lone ferryman Charon who crosses this boundary continually, who is also described as a rough, coarse being. To take people across the boundary of acceptability into the eerie, the strange and unknown is indeed hard, thankless work most of the time, because people rarely appreciate the uncomfortable situation of being taken to a world, or a view of their world that they do not know how to handle or react to.

If we apply our One Point of View to this situation, the scene at the river's edge makes a lot of sense. Remember that from the Key Point of View, there is only a dimensionless Point of Awareness, and everything else is the loving companion to that awareness, including our own mind and the entire universe around us. This is a description of our true nature, whole and complete.

Whenever we reject anything in our environment, we are deliberately ignoring part of our world, part of reality. Styx means hate, or rejection. This river of rejection is one of the greatest divisions in our whole world, encircling the underworld and the entire Universe nine times in total, making nine divisions therein. On one hand, these divisions in our world allow for definition, specialization, and concentration of our efforts, allowing for experimentation, study, growth and evolution, much like the successive veils in a mystery religion do. But on the other hand, what we don't like or can't handle is off limits to us, even though things may be in reality an intimate part of our immediate experience. In order to reject anything, even for the sake of being able to concentrate, we have to ignore a lot about what we reject, and about ourselves too;

we have to "shove it under the carpet". This is how so much of our world gets buried behind veils of ignoring, or ignorance. Unfortunately, out of sight is also out of mind, and we eventually forget that we are ignoring what we ignore, and we forget that we forgot. Of the rejected universe, the Underworld, all we see is that is "difficult", the stuff we don't want to talk about, the things that make us uncomfortable, and the issues we don't want anything to do with, even if we really forget why.

If we don't know we're really gods on earth, that we are living in Nirvan here and now, if we don't know how to act like who we really are, it's because the things we're forgetting, the things we need to know and do are hidden in the things we ignore and reject, the things we don't like. The very happiness we all search continually for, the wealth of Hades, is to be found across that hateful river, in the foreboding realms of the Underworld. In this sense, the river Styx is the Abyss... we are only as far from Enlightenment as the width of this river, the distance from those things we reject.

The wraiths at the water's edge, with no conscious volition of their own (being dead) cannot approach what they automatically fear or hate. This fear and hate is for them a boundary they have no power to overcome and cross. The fear and the hate are deep and swift, cold and dark, and threaten to swallow up and drown anyone who might try to ford or swim in it's current and undercurrents of violence. Yet everything they want is on the other side, whatever happiness means for each of them, is what they've exiled into their Underworld. All they need is to forget their prejudice and recognize that which they reject to be the very object of their desire... all they need do to cross the boundary is to love more strongly than they hate or fear. We, as mystics, have the ability to provide the merit/love to those that cannot find for them selves, because love and acceptance is contagious... and the wraiths, with no volition of their own (being dead) are defenseless against such infection.

CERBERUS: The Dweller on the Threshold

"As above, so below" and we have our own personal boundaries of acceptability. There is a line within our minds between what we care to think about and what we'd rather ignore, for whatever reasons. We artificially divide our minds into two unequal parts. There is the smaller "conscious" part comprised of the comfortable and acceptable thoughts, motivations, plans, ideas, memories, attitudes, and perceptions. There is also that vast and mysterious subconscious part of ourselves comprised of everything we don't want to know about because they make us uncomfortable for various reasons. It may be that we are uncomfortable with something we don't understand, and therefore do not trust, and would rather ignore whatever makes us worry in this way. There may be painful memories, terribly embarrassing associations, painful or embarrassing mistakes we can't fix, or problems too huge to do anything about. There may be more subtle problems that we ourselves create, and push out of our awareness or ignore.

At the same time, our own true nature, so vast, complex and incomprehensible, literally mind boggling, is also "shoved under the carpet" like the proverbial "baby thrown out with the bath-water", because it is, simply mind-boggling.

Cerberus, then, is what we look like when we enforce and defend this artificial separation between the living and the dead, the conscious and unconscious – what we want to know about and what we don't want to know about.

A description of his parents tells us where and why we first developed this power of discrimination:

Here follows an analysis of the description of Derberus's Father, Typhoeus:

Myth: "Cerberus's father…"
English: The seed or need for this quality called Cerberus arises from…

Myth: "… was a Titan, one of Gaia's sons."
English: …a primitive aspect of our nature, indeed, of all creation, even space itself.

Myth: "Typhoeus was the biggest and strongest of all of Gaia's children."
English: This is the strongest characteristic of the mind…

Myth: "His arms reach through the dark part of the universe, from dusk to dawn…"
English: … the unconscious, or instinctive, automatic and all-pervasive tendency or compulsion to…

Myth: "…His lower body is shaped like two wrestling serpents…"
English: … cling to whatever arises in the mind, considering it as one's own, and even as oneself, and then even grasping at and wrestling with that idea of a "self," wrestling with oneself…

Myth: "…and he has a hundred heads sprouting from his shoulders, and his body is covered with wings.."
English: …making the vastness of naked experience simply to much to comprehend all at once with all its myriad ideas and complex principals.

Myth: "Hissing and bellowing, he flung fiery stones at Heaven and from his mouth spurted flames instead of spittle."
English: This incomprehensibility of all we are, and all we want to keep track of and own, is ugly, unsettling, unproductive, and disruptive, even painful and confusing at times.

Myth: "Zeus subdued him finally by throwing a huge mountain on him, and thus confined him to the Underworld,…"
English: To establish some order in our perception and our lives, we use the stability of physical perception to ignore the huge, unmanageable bulk of our true nature. This is a method of ignoring by shifting attention to a stable physical perception.

Myth: "…but he still sometimes hurls fiery stones and flames from that mountain, which we call today, mount

Etna."
English: Even so, from time to time, we are disturbed by unsettling reminders of the awesome power that lies hidden beneath our artificial face, or surface.

Here follows an analysis of the description of Derberus's Mother, Echidna:

Myth: "Cerberus's Mother…"
English: A solution to this problem (represented by the father, Typhoeus) was given birth…

Myth: "… was also a Titan…"
English: …by another automatic function inherent in our primal nature…

Myth: "…daughter of the "Old Ones of the Sea", Phorkys and Keto."
English: …the ocean-like vastness and depth of our own minds…"

Myth: "…Her name was Echidna, meaning "serpent".
English: …seems to engulf, swallow and appropriate whatever it's aware of, like water pervading, enveloping and dissolving whatever is dropped into it.

Myth: "She is half beautiful woman…"
English: This is the soothing, attractive…

Myth: "…half serpent with a masculine disposition."
English: …primitive, automatic, reptile-like, though almost intentional, tendency…

Myth: "She lives in a cave far from gods and men…"
English: …to take advantage of the fact that whatever is "out of sight" is also "out of mind".

Myth: "…and devours her victims raw."
English: By appropriating and digesting something, making it part of ourselves, we no longer see the thing in our environment. This is a method of ignoring by internalizing. By making something an automatic habit, we need no longer be aware of it, and soon forget about it, even though it is deeply buried in our nature. The holiest quality of the Universe is it's infinite curiosity, its Desire for experience, for Love, Life and Light. This curiosity is the Goddess Hecate in all of us, it is the true Spirit of humanity that shall see us survive through the end of eternity. We are the Universe itself, vast and ineffable, and in order to become conscious of itself, to see itself through its own eyes, we the Universe restrict our view to that of a tiny, specialized creature, living a tiny specialized life on the face of a tiny specialized speck of dust. To satisfy its infinite curiosity and Desire for experience, the Universe does this from countless billions upon billions of very special "Points of View", from as many "Points of View" as there are points of light in the sky.

Faced with the confusingly infinite possibilities of every instant of existence, we use the qualities of Hecate (Echidna) and Typhon to ignore the most of it so we can concentrate on what we do know, on what we can handle, so we can specialize and deal with the experience of existence carefully one step at a time. "Pain is the

Universe Growing" and we have developed ways to reduce the pain to manageable levels in order to survive. This is the secret of the "ring-pass-not" and of the magical axiom: "there is power in restriction".

Thus, we have developed a three headed watch-dog: selective perception, selective memory, and inhibitions through the union of Hecate (Echidna) and Typhon, two self-serving methods of ignoring, for the sake of maintaining the illusion: for survival. We have developed a convenient and natural tendency to shun that which is disturbing and counter-productive to our comfort, our survival and our growth.

Once we have accomplished this Self-restriction, the Universe "turns about in the seat of consciousness" and starts to look at Itself from each unique angle, and the Universe marvels at the wonder of what It sees with each successive discovery of Itself, in the process of self-discovery, the process we call the third way to travel the Paths: every-day experience.

Or so it goes in a perfect world.

When the Universe, thinking it is a tiny and insignificant, begins to explore itself, becomes self-conscious and sees a little of itself that Reminds it of its own true nature too quickly for comfortable comprehension, when it sees clues that might destroy the whole illusion of being a tiny, insignificant creature, and thus "spoil the fun" and threaten "survival", we can and do use our ability to ignore the facts, even when they are staring us right in the face. We become experts at guarding the Underworld, keeping the conscious, living things in the daylight of waking life, and keeping the things we don't want to know about deep underground, out of sight, banished from our concern along with the rest of the universe we can't quite handle yet.

Every time we wake up in the morning, when we've had enough rest and decide to perform the next act in the on-going play of our lives, we have to invoke Cerberus to re-establish the boundary between what we're going to be aware of, and what we're not going to be aware of today. We forget much of what went on all night. At first we don't even remember who we are, having been no-one and everyone for several hours. Then we successively remember and re-establish our "character" like an actor warming up before an appearance, or like the Jackal headed Anubis at the start of every magical operation, proclaiming the magical intention, guarding the confines of the temple, and banishing irrelevant thoughts and spirits.

Cerberus is invoked whenever we sneeze, have an orgasm, faint, or otherwise "pass unconscious". The fact is, it is impossible to be "unconscious". "Awareness" is what existence feels like, and as long as Anything exists, that's how it feels. Since we cannot escape being That which exists, we cannot escape being Aware. What we can do, though, is ignore. So when we say we were "unconscious", we really mean we are ignoring what we were aware of, and even ignoring that we were perfectly aware the whole time.

When we do this, we are lying, just as we lie every time we deliberately act in ignorance. We have a quality in our nature, a basic part of our make-up that allows us to exist as we are, that lies continually about what we see, what we think and do, and what we are.

The interesting thing is that this quality of our basic make-up has to be aware of both sides of the fence... it has to know "this is something we don't want out in the open" and "this other thing is something we don't want meddling with taboo". This aspect of our own minds therefore knows all the secrets we hide from ourselves, from the awesome vastness of our heritage as the Universe itself, to the dirtiest little "skeletons in the closet". It is no surprise then, to find that "Cerberus" translates as Guard the Secret".

The act of such ignoring and secret-keeping is not a simple one. To keep a secret from ourselves, we can't be aware of keeping the secret, can we? The keeper of secrets must then itself be a secret. The guardian of the Underworld must himself be banished to the Underworld. He must operate independently of our conscious awareness, like a servant, but because he is an integral part of our own mind, he will by nature be as loyal as a pet dog, anticipating his master's every wish, watching his master for clues as to "friend" or "foe", "attack" or "welcome". He has to do his job alone, automatically, like the primitive, automatic, involuntary, reptilian part of our brain. Without his master's direct "conscious" command he has to swallow up what we don't want to think about, and scare us away from approaching secret things we don't want to know or think about. Because he only has the primitive, automatic, involuntary, reptilian part of our brain to work with, it might seem as though he were a cross between a dog and a reptile or serpent.

To make things worse, our faithful guard dog has to watch with intelligence and deliberation, simultaneously, what we see outside, what we think inside, and what we do about it. He has to know the truth and the lies on each of these three fronts, and simultaneously censor all three of them, almost as though he were required to have three independent heads at once.

When the Universe, thinking it is tiny and insignificant, has forgotten it's reason for forgetting (to make the show convincing to itself) it has also forgotten the facts and the values and the implications that go with who it really is and the nature of this reality. The facts and values we forget are that everyone and everything around us is really a reflection of ourselves, and that when something happens to someone else, it is really happening to ourselves.

Not knowing who we really are, we make "mistakes", and we hurt other people, and we hurt ourselves. Sometimes we can't face the pain we have caused or have seen in someone else, because it hints of how close we really are to that person. The powerful sympathy that naturally arises for someone's pain can be so intense, and so intimate that it rivals sex as an experience of unity. When such strong feelings of unity threaten our confidence as individuals, threaten our illusion of being a whole and complete entity in ourselves, we feel like our survival as individuals is also threatened. We react to this breach of individuality as though it were a threat to our survival and our loving Cerberus tries his best to ease our anguish and swallow up any reminders of the incident, and tries to frighten us away from thinking about it, doing anything about it, or even remembering it even happened. Sometimes Cerberus can be so clever as to remove the pain from the act of hurting someone while we perform the act itself! It is possible for us to hurt someone and ignore the fact even while we do it, and it's remarkable how like an enraged dog people act when this happens... any hint of weakness or fear in the victim, any reminder of the pain and suffering one is causing evokes more rage to try to drown it out with. As mentioned before, There may be problems in our lives that we ourselves create, and push out of our awareness or ignore, such as the inability to face facts about one's appearance, or facts about one's personal habits. When someone (a lover or a teacher) loves us very much, and cares for us enough to try to help with these aspects of ourselves that we don't know how to handle, and don't want to deal with, like Cerberus we turn on them with wrath, venom and threats. We end up severely hurting the ones that love us most, the ones that are closest to our hearts.

The whole situation gets messy as more and more of our lives are ignored, the lies we tell ourselves get more and more complex, self-contradictory, and more difficult to carry. Whenever we suppress something of importance, it doesn't really go away... you can't say something doesn't exist just because you're not aware of it, and you can't say you don't feel a certain way just because you don't want to admit it or think about it, and you can't say you don't do something just because you don't want to admit it... it's there all the time nonetheless. Now when you deny something that's important to you, something about which there are constant reminders to be "swallowed", to keep up appearances, we have to act like the reminders aren't really there either. We become neurotic, trying to continually deny that we know something is there, and start to act strangely, in ways that don't make sense. These neuroses, these on-going lies each become a burden of on-going automatic maintenance. It's as though Cerberus sprouts a serpent head on his back for each neurotic behaviour pattern he must carry, and eventually the burden is heavy on his back. The serpent heads, each chattering their own lies, greedily vying for more attention, sometimes contradicting each other and fighting among each other, become something too loud to ignore, too heavy to bear. It's no wonder we need to take a rest from trying to be who we think we are... the burden is heavy and we need our sleep.

It's at this point where we become aware that there's a lot more to reality than we think, and we start to wonder just what the truth is. The louder the mental chatter of serpents jealously proclaiming their own version of the truth, the less inner peace we have... the more tiring the whole game is, the more we wonder what the truth really is. At this point, we are like Persephone in the oldest version of her myth, where she lives in a dark cave all her life, unaware of the vastness of the world around her, spending her time spinning wool. Eventually she spins so much wool that she gets all tangled up in it, and her whole world is caught up in this tiny part of the cave, with it's own tiny drama of problems and solutions, but all bound up in the mess of wool she herself has spun. She knows nothing of a "normal" life in the bright outside world around her, and she knows nothing of love, being a virgin, and want's nothing to do with it either, being incomprehensible to her. Out of love and concern for her poor "spinster" daughter, knowing the fullness of life she is missing, Demeter approaches a great and powerful god, Zeus of the Underworld, with whom she knows Persephone has a lot in common and whom she knows Persephone will respect and eventually love. She arranges to have him come to the cave and carry her off to be his wife. Of course, to Persephone, this is kidnap and rape, but eventually, she loosens up, breaks out of her old life and finds love and power through him.

It's at this point where we've fooled Ourselves too well, and the lies and self-deception begin to harm Us and Others instead of concentrate Us for growth. It's at this point where the restriction must be broken, and We must now explore Our true nature from this imaginary "View-Point" that has taken Us so long to create. The illusion is as "real" as it can get.

Now it takes courage and "strength" to bring Cerberus out into the open and expose the lies and fact him and befriend him, not to be afraid of him. But all he can do is try to frighten you from the things you are hiding (from), he won't harm you because, after all, he is Hecate's servant, and Hecate is his master... he loves you and this is the only reason he does his job... he loves you because he is indeed part of you.

The secret to "Facing the Dweller On the Threshold", Cerberus, is in the Key to the Path... in that constant Awareness which is your true nature, unshakeable like a mountain, illuminating enlightening like Hecate. By resting there, as that One Point of View, you are no longer an insignificant human to be scared away from the underworld with threats of madness... you are the disciple of the "Mother", and you have the powers of Hecate to pass Cerberus without fear... after all, who is he going to frighten?

CERBERUS THE DOG: "Man's Best Friend"

If you look at Cerberus without fear, what do you see" A faithful servant and pet, who knows all the secrets there are to know about you, and who loves you anyway, and who only ever wanted to protect you from fear and pain. The secrets he keeps from you out of love are only kept so because he senses your discomfort and wants you to be happy. But if you have the courage and the peace of mind to face the facts, found only in that One Point of View, and you are not afraid of the secrets Cerberus keeps, then he can be the most knowledgeable guide to your inner secret self that you can find. And after being left alone to do his job in the Underworld for so long, faithfully doing his duty out of love for you, he would dance and bark and run like a puppy at the opportunity to play with you and be your friend. With all his aeons of experience with illusions and secrets, the possibilities for games of hide-and-seek, games of surprise, wit and hidden meanings with such a creature could be some of the most amusing and rewarding pastimes in your life. At the same time he has the power to keep us from ever confusing illusion with reality again, like Hecate, the Black Bitch who became Persephone's constant companion and priestess after she returned from the depths of the Underworld as it's Queen.

It is for these reasons that when we first meet Cerberus in the Underworld, he is quite threatening, first held in check by his master as we are his guests, then later he is unleashed and we have to face him alone. It is also for these reasons that the key to getting past Cerberus is to hold your fear in check, for as with most guard dogs, the slightest act of fear or anger enrages the beast. Then, when Cerberus is sure you are not a threat, that you are willing to accept what he has to show you, when he is sure that you "Wish to Know In Order to Serve", and that you are "Willing to Suffer In Order To Learn", he becomes your guide. When you are willing to look in the mirror and face yourself completely without acting out of fear for all the aspects of yourself, all the way from the view of the petty, ugly little secrets you may keep from yourself and others, to the view of your true heritage as a conscious incarnation of the Universe itself, then you become the Lord and

Master of the Underworld yourself. Perhaps you are like Persephone, at first horrified by the awesome display of what you see, at being wrenched from your comfortable, small, and predictable life, but later released on the infinite shores of your Cosmic Nature, embraced in the arms of your eternal loving companion: the play of life and death.

All this is fine in beautiful journeys in our psychic imagination, but in the real world we have to be ruthlessly honest with ourselves, and we have to go to our own underworld often, befriend our own personal Cerberus and teach him to swallow our pride and our fear instead of the truth. We have to learn all he has to teach about ourselves, saying to ourselves: whenever there's something scary, or uncomfortable to think about, or something we hate; that's one of Cerberus's secrets, that's one of Cerberus's lessons, and that's something we need very much to learn about, and learn from... it's one of those things we've split off from ourselves, the infinite beings that we really are, and one of the things we need to get back, to know who we are, and act like we are whole and infinite still. In this sense, we need to develop the strength of character and "power" of Hercules to be able to face those most terrifying, embarrassing, disillusioning, disheartening, hope-shattering things, as well as the awesomely beautiful, frighteningly wonderful, and unbearably precious things about ourselves. In this sense, we need to develop strength of character if we are really to know and understand and love ourselves and each other the way we really are — which is the whole point to path-working in the first place. It will take all of the qualities, and lessons, and strength we build with worshipping Hecate to do this. Hecate devotees have an enormous advantage to handle the path and release fear entirely. Hecate may not be the "Queen of the Underworld" but she is the priestess of the underworld. This means she is the wisdom of the underworld. Hecate being the priestess of the underworld controls all the knowledge of Hades and Persephone is her right hand. No force can illumine your real self, take you through the shadows like my Queen, Hecate! (Hecate/Echnida equation verified in "Hecate II: The Awakening of Hydra.)

Hecate Art

Hecate Brimo

Hecate Triceps

Hecate Luna

Hecate Lucifera

Hecate Sol

Hecate Trivia

Hecate Scorpio
ARTWORK by Bobbie James

Jade Sol Luna

Hecate Devotee and Astrologer Jade Sol Luna has traveled extensively in his 14-year quest to unravel the various forms of Ancient Astrology. Jade gives sessions with the form of Lunar Astrology that was practiced by the Ancient Greeks and Roman and is the only U.S.-based astrologer who practices "Astrologia Lunaris". Luna has written his unique form of astrological practice in various magazines, including Hinduism Today and Whole Life Times and has been featured on numerous radio and TV shows including Sedona talk Radio and runs his own radio show "Night Ritual" on PRN Network. Jade Luna has released his first book "Hecate", and is writing his second called "Astrologia Lunaris", based upon the oldest system of Astrology in the Mediterranean that may have well influenced the modern system of Hindu Astrology called Jyotish. This Ancient Mediterranean, Sidereal system prioritizes the Moon and the 27 lunar mansions above the 12 solar signs. Jade Luna's seminars on Astrology and ancient Roman mystical paths are in demand across the United States and around the world. He also has owns his own Ambient Record Label, JSL INC.

JADE SOL LUNA on JSLINC. Records

CD-Scorpio Invocatio

The Third CD release from the team of Jade Luna and Jordan James on Legatus Records. This is a strong meditative chant that takes the listener deep into the constellation Scorpio, the home of the Greek Goddess Hecate. Deep droning undertones create a soundscape of intensity and transformation. Not your typical meditative CD, but something very real and original. A must for those that want to explore the deep subconscious.

CD-Zodiac Hymns

Another Jade Luna and Jordan James collection of Ambient chanting Cd's on CreateS Records. This CD is Pre-Augustas Latin Chanting to the Planetary Gods. It is an Ambient CD mixed with Egyptian and Greek undertones. Awesome for meditations that take you back to Ancient Rome and Greece.

CD-Silver Moon, Black Sun

This Dark Ambient CD is a collection of the most powerful Latin, Greek and Demotic Hymns known. The tracks on these CD's can be used for overcoming fear, house clearings, the removing of negative energies, empowering stones, gaining inner strength, and most important... to invoke the power of the Feminine Divine!

Also, just released! **HECATE PHANTASMAGORIA** and **QUEEN OF THE CROSSROADS**
Buy or www.jslinc.org

Special Thanks to Jana for assisting in this work and to the Great Mother Hecate for her love and inspiration. Also a special thanks to Solar Culture Gallery, The Albuquerque Group, Santa Fe Soul, Avatar Meher Baba, Ramakrishna, my mother Karen Webber, Sky Webber (The Buddha) for his strength, My father for his love of nature, James Lee, Adam (Noctifer), Matt and Bobbie James, The Healing Essence Center, Salem Underground, Hinduism Today, Wiccan Promotions, Legatus Records.

NOTES:

NOTES:

INDIA RESEARCH PRESS / TARA PRESS INTERNATIONAL

INDIA

Corporate Office -
B-4/22,Khajuraho - 110 029, INDIA
Telephone :   91-11-2369 4610 Telefax :   91-11-2471 8637

Editorial Office -

Flat #6, TRUST OFFICE - 110003, India.
Tel: 00.91.11.2469 4610, 2469 4855
TeleFAX: 00.91.11.24618637, 417 57 113

AMERICA

JSL INC Press.
14431 Ventura Blvd suite 538
Sherman Oaks CA 91423
www.hiddenmoon.com

www.ingramcontent.com/pod-product-compliance
Lightning Source LLC
Chambersburg PA
CBHW020648300426
44112CB00007B/292